I DON'T LIKE TO COMPLAIN, BUT...

it IS what I'm best at

Copyright © 2017 by James Manns. All rights reserved.

ISBN-13: 978-1-936936-11-3
Published by
Avventura Press
133 Handley St.
Eynon PA 18403-1305
www.avventurapress.com

First printing January 2017
Printed in the United States of America

What people are saying about I Don't Like to Complain, but it *IS* What I'm Best At

"If you're in the mood for a delightful dose of sarcasm, innuendo, fierce and curmudgeonly observations, delicious absurdities, and downright lunacy, you have come to the right place. Author and philosopher Jim Manns delves into the weirdness and glory of life on this planet. His take on things sparkles with wit and keen intelligence."

—*Dennis Corrigan*
Assistant Professor
Art Department
Marywood University

"Professor Manns takes us on an insightful and amusing jaunt through modern life, with stops along the way to consider what Las Vegas and academic journals have in common, why movie ratings have it backwards, and why, with any luck, you'll be dead before your troubles catch up to you. Manns' voice is smart and congenial, and at once familiar—just the kind of guide you want for this journey."

—*Steven Heiner*
Adjunct Professor of Philosophy
North Carolina State University

In fourteen lively essays philosopher James Manns applies his rare wit to a variety of timely topics—the end of sex (as we knew it), movie ratings for "mature" adults, the dispensability of iPhones, how to catch rats and release hummingbirds in La Jolla, on being American in France, basketball here and abroad, American vs. French waiters, and many others. His fresh insights are served up with a delicious humor reminiscent of Mark Twain and Will Rogers.

—*Alan Perreiah*
Professor of Philosophy
University of Kentucky

Only James Manns could discover the Newtonian and Einsteinian dimensions of basketball, or use that same sport to explain differences between American and French attitudes toward food. You'll have to read I Don't Like to Complain to learn how he reaches these and many other keen and far-reaching connections, for they aren't to be found anywhere else.

—*Edward Stanton*
Author, *Wide As the Wind*

I DON'T LIKE TO COMPLAIN, BUT...

it IS what I'm best at

ESSAYS ON TOPICS SMALL AND SMALLER YET

JAMES MANNS

AVVENTURA PRESS

CONTENTS

INTRODUCTION	13
MA-LSV	21
DEAR GLORIA	33
KNOWLEDGE IS . . . BORING	37
THE LAST HURRAH (AN AMERICAN TRAGEDY?)	41
WITH ANY LUCK . . .	51
THE END OF SEX (AS WE KNEW IT)	57
TROUBLE IN PARADISE	63
PRIVATE ENEMY NUMBER ONE	67
BEAR WITH ME (TO THE END)	77
NOTES ON THE IMPOSSIBLE	83
DE GUSTIBUS	101
SKETCHBOOK	113
IDLE-IZE ME!	131
THE OLYMPIC EXPERIENCE	137

For

DENNIS CORRIGAN
whose artistic brilliance long inspired me
and whose earnest encouragement sustained me
in this effort

SPECIAL THANKS

To my wife Syham, who stands in the foreground
or the background of all these pieces, and who for years
encouraged me to commit them to paper
"in my own special way."

And to Lee Sebastiani, who from day one of our
acquaintance has been all encouragement, and whose
expertise has led to the book which you now
hold in hand.

To-morrow, and to-morrow, (=/=) and to-morrow, (=/=)
Creeps in this petty pace from day to day, (=/=)
To the last syllable of recorded time; (=/o)
And all our yesterdays have lighted fools
The way to dusty death. (o/o) Out, out brief candle! (o/o)
Life's but a walking shadow; (=/=)

IF SHAKESPEARE HAD EMOTICONS

Introduction

Who? When? Where?

It was suggested that, being something less than a household word (like, e.g., "mildew"?), to say a few words about who I am and what I am about here would be in order. Pretty close to the toughest topic I've ever been assigned to write on, perhaps I can make it easy by making it short. So here goes.

I was born just at the tail end of the second and last intramundane conflict—the war that couldn't fail to end all wars; we're sure to get it right this time, second time's a charm. So had I, at birth (*per impossibile*), enjoyed a reasonable level of meaningful cognition, I would surely have recognized that my life was destined to unfold during a peace that could not but endure forever.

Or for five years, whichever came first.

During those five years it turned out, with my father being in the military, that I had more addresses than I was to have for the remainder of my life—though most of them came and went before I had developed any concept of "place." From the Boston area (where I debuted as a person), to Corpus Christi, Texas, to Santa Ana, California, back to Rockland (Mass., the first place I actually became aware of as "home"), then on to Toms River, NJ (proximate to Lakehurst Naval Air Station), where we bounced from one temporary domicile to another until finally settling in on—how idyllic!—Maple Street, my permanent address for the next fifteen years.

When I tell people that Toms River was a great place to be *from*, I intend the remark to be dual-edged: It was a great place to *be* at that given time, a peaceful, rustic setting to grow up in (there were eagles' nests atop telephone poles in my early—pre DDT—years there!). There was a broadening river two blocks away (yes, the Toms River—no apostrophe—and a good thing, that, as who knows where to put an apostrophe anymore?), an ocean close by, and the Pine Barrens immediately to the south. It had an excellent school system and, what I only came to appreciate later in life, an interesting amalgam of ethnicities, most of them recent arrivals—swept over to our shores by that hideous European conflict which only recently had ended. But with the creeping urbanization afflicting the whole Boston-to-Washington corridor, and all that that entailed, our "charming small town" came to be small no more, and lost its charm.

Then the chemical company moved in and poisoned the waters. I still have a vivid memory of our mayor dipping a glass into the Toms River and drinking the contents, to prove to all residents how safe the clean-up had rendered it. Ah, what joys must come with political commitment! I wonder how he—or his *progeny*—fared in the years following that "public spirited display"? Did those tales of a mysterious denizen of the Pines known as the Jersey Devil at last find some real life embodiment?! In any case, "a good place to be *from*" came to imply, to my way of seeing things, "but never to return *to*."

My first step on the way to extricating myself from south Jersey was a normal four-year stretch at a small college—Lafayette College—just across the Delaware. When I arrived there I had no idea that this was the environment in which I would be spending most of the rest of my life. When it came to selecting a major, though, the decision

Introduction

didn't come easily. I had gone, supposedly, to prepare for a career in engineering, but an unhappy confrontation with the second derivative soured me quickly on that. The English Dept. was heavily oversubscribed; the college simply had no music major; ultimately I settled on Philosophy—and thus in this fateful manner did the forces of the cosmos align themselves to give birth to a career!

After four years at this all-boys' college (I balk at calling my fellow students there "men"), on the hill overlooking Easton, PA (home of boxing great Larry Holmes and ... anybody else?), I headed off to Boston for graduate study—in that order of importance: it was my primary aim to experience life in a civilized metropolis; along the way maybe I could pick up an advanced degree in Philosophy, too. This latter intention, however, was to founder early on—was it Philosophy or Boston that was proving too much for me? Whichever, after one semester in the program, it simply didn't feel like it was "me," and I dropped out. The "me" in question, I think, was someone with an aching social conscience—a fairly common affliction in the late '60s, one that was to be, some would say, "cured," though I would prefer *dismantled* during the Reagan years.

But then something wondrous happened! Before the next fall semester rolled around (*just* before!) I found myself married, and a joyous new phase of life had opened up, with but one limitation, to wit: I had no real job and no prospects for one. That social conscience, my deep commitment to solving the problems of the world, empowering the voiceless, épatée-ing the *bourgeoisie*, and other such noble causes, suddenly ran afoul of my need to become serious about gainful employment. *Responsibility* knocked *thunderously*. What choice had I but to attempt to run a finesse on this sticky situation and—don't laugh now! Nary a snicker!—*return to Philosophy*, this time with career aspirations.

For this endeavor I owe a great debt of thanks to Prof. Walter Emge at Boston University. Students were allowed to remain in the graduate program with two grades below B—a third would result in termination—and in that first semester I "earned" one C and received one Incomplete (which, incidentally, remains to this day incomplete; I wonder, does the statute of limitations kick in after 50 years?). Then there was Prof. Emge's Medieval Philosophy class. I wrote a paper for it that I knew at the time (and I have not subsequently revised that judgment) deserved at best a D-. And yet he gave me a B! It is impossible to say what would have become of me if he had given me what I deserved, but it is pretty safe to say I would not be where I am now, writing this. In any case, my candidacy still had a pulse to it, and once the spur of necessity provided me with ample motivation, completing the degree became, while far from easy, at least doable. And I did it.

Four years later, in early June, I defended my dissertation in the morning and boarded a plane for France in the afternoon (a Pan Am, to give some sense of the long-ago-ness; to give even a better sense, we were given menus to select our in-flight dinners from, and wine was of course complimentary). Early the next morning I stepped off the plane in Paris, nursing a serious migraine (the pressure of the defense and its subsequent release, combined with all that complimentary wine seem to have been at fault), but entering a grand new phase of life.

I had succeeded, in landing a tenure track position at the University of Kentucky in Lexington, an attractive city (or really a very big town—since then it has grown into a very *very* big town) in the Bluegrass region, ringed by the most glorious horse farms America has to offer. My trials in securing this position were as light as could be, as my interview with their department was the only one I had to endure, and it proved to be the *last* one I would have to endure. An entire academic career growing out of one single interview, at a respectable school, in a reasonably appealing locale—today's candidates could only shake their heads in bitter disbelief at such a revelation!

For the next 32 years I engaged in the usual professorial and academic activities, even managing a trip or two dozen abroad (that initial, celebratory trip to France proved most fruitful, leading even to a small real estate investment in Paris that served us handsomely for two decades), before taking an early retirement—"early" in bureaucratic or chronometric time; "not a moment too soon" in felt, psychological time.

My early years spent abreast of the ocean had grown increasingly fond in memory, though, as Lexington must be one of the few cities of its size, in this (or any) country, that has no proximity to water. There isn't even a river that runs through it, or around it. The Kentucky River is a good 20 miles to the west, the Ohio an hour and a half to the north (by Cincinnati, and northwest, where it passes alongside Louisville). Retirement provided me with the opportunity to relocate and renew my acquaintance with the salt water, and as a consequence I find myself writing this from a desk that would provide me with a glimpse of the Pacific—if only that marine layer would lift!—in the beautiful town of La Jolla (pronounced "La Jolla"), California, a suburb of San Diego. (Remember my calling Lexington a very *very* big town? Well, San Diego is an *enormous* big town.)

So there, in this era when there is talk of speed dating, I hereby offer a bit of speed biographizing—my life in a nutshell. In fact, as I'm sure goes on in the dating realm as well, I appear to have provided *nothing but* the nutshell, though my shell probably fits the nut more snugly than theirs, where doubtless many a peanut is paraded about as if it were a pecan. (But just incidentally, far from being a recent and novel phenomenon, isn't speed dating largely what was going on in those balls of a couple/few centuries ago—those that Jane Austen so carefully, frequently, and lovingly depicted in her novels? The role of the modern timepiece was assumed back then by the orchestra, and as dance followed dance, so too did brief encounter follow brief encounter. Everyone knew and abided by the rules. It's just a thought, anyway.)

Now if only some—any!—of the foregoing shed even the slightest bit of light on the following!

Why? How?

Some, there are—many of them, in fact—who believe that a sufficiently detailed accounting of the external factors in one's life can shed valuable, critical light on the inner workings of that person's mind. George Marek is hardly alone on a limb when he declares in his biography of Beethoven (provocatively titled *Beethoven*) "I see Beethoven as a man who grew from the soil of his times and stood deep in the cultural, political, and social streams that swirled around him . . . I have attempted to show [him] in the cocoon of his times and trace the progress of chrysalis into genius [p. xiii]."

Well, I waded through all 640 pages of that soil (which grew pretty muddy—clumpy--at times thanks to those streams of culture and politics swirling over it). No doubt I stepped on a few cocoons along the way, but I never could see how those environing conditions led to the musical genius—the Beethoven of Opus 111—whom we so deeply revere. I'm not holding Marek blameworthy here, except perhaps for fancying that he could succeed in an undertaking *where everyone else before him had failed.* For I suggest that the people whose behavior, beliefs, their very *being* can be resolved into a network of social, cultural, *external* factors, are precisely the kind of people whom we regard as—how can I put this politely? I can't!—flat out boring. And who wants to take the trouble to write a biography of a painfully boring person (then try to market it)?

You might think the task had some possibility of reaching fulfillment if the subject in question was a non-genius, like, for example, me. In a case like that the leaps from facts to fancy might not be so broad and perilous as for a Beethoven. But they have proven too much for *me* to make. My little bit of auto-geography above might tell you (and me) where I've been on the surface of the globe, and when, but not where my thoughts have been, there and then. John Locke assures us that our soul is to be found wherever our body is, and if we travel from Oxford to London, our soul makes the same trip "as the coach or horse does that carries [us]." So playing along with Locke, my soul (or mind or "thinking substance") did indeed happen to be in all those places I described above; yet what it happened to be *thinking*, at any time in its spatial trajectory, was, well, its own business, and as often as not might have been found in a galaxy far, far away.

And introspect as hard as I can, finding the algorithm that would explain why I write the things I write, and why I write them that way, seems forever to elude me, leaving me—despite the privileged access introspection is supposed to provide—feeling as if, like Little Anthony (fronting his Imperials), "I'm on the outside (looking in)"! And it's a *very* dark glass I'm looking through. So perhaps the matter at hand should be turned on its head, and instead of introducing myself so that you may better sympathize with what I have written, it will turn out that what I have written will better enable you to locate (and sympathize with) who I am.

The several drawings that are scattered through the articles here are equally mysterious (to me) in origin. I'll be looking at something and suddenly a fusion is made—I find myself giggling, and a cartoon is born. Well, at least it is *conceived*. The birthing process has been an entirely separate matter. I've heard of actual births that stretched into the *second day*, from the initial warning signal to the emergence of the Bundle of Joy. A few of these cartoons, however, did not achieve realization—poke into the sunlit world—until the second or *third decade* after their appearance in mind! There is a mechanical aspect to any drawing—a technique: there are some right ways and many wrong ways to achieve a representation of an idea held in mind. And while Leonardo, say, may have been in control of this technique intuitively or instinctively, I certainly wasn't. Hence it wasn't until I had retired and was able to devote sizable chunks of time to a drawing class (a night class at UCSD) and the lessons that followed from it that I was able to make a meaningful stab at giving shape to my ideas. (Some of them still puzzle me: anyone who has a clear sense of which character (p. 82) *is* Mr. Petit Mal and which *is* Mr. Grand Mal, please contact me at your earliest convenience.)

This humble volume represents the first time I have been able to write about subjects and issues that have directly and immediately pressed themselves upon my consciousness and craved verbal expression; *and* which I have felt free to express in a manner, a style that has been unfettered by "professional proprieties" (hoo-hah!). My academic career did oblige me to write things—two books, a couple dozen articles (a modest output)—but the format, content, and style of composition that comes out of this period was imposed on me by that horrifying cadre of blind (and often deaf and dumb, and not infrequently mean-spirited) reviewers, as well as by market considerations—yes, amazingly there are market factors at work in academic literature. Even in Philosophy! But here I have granted license to the individual chapters to write themselves, in the manner they see fit.

I was told at various times in my teaching career that students unfamiliar with my "delivery" would wonder aloud, or ask one another "Is he serious or what?" It is my hope that no such questions arise in the pages that follow, but just in case you should find a doubt or two creeping in at some point, I have a simple answer ready in advance, to wit: "No, I'm not serious; except at some level I *am*; at least I *think* I am—actually it all depends on what you mean by "*serious*." So now that I've cleared that up, I urge: If laughter be the spice of life, read on.

I do offer my apologies, however, to those of you who consider yourselves to be part of the "modern audience," for my inability to have worked any gratuitous vulgarity into these essays. I know how central this element is to recent literature (and cinema, and television, always providing knee-jerk, faintly nervous laughs), and it is my hope that you will not be too offended by this deficit. But if at any time you suffer palpitations or shortness of breath for want of some duly tasteless stimulation, normally involving some mention of genitalia, fear not: a life-saving infusion of same is readily available by simply tapping a couple keys—I'm sure you know which ones--on that little phone-like computer contraption, you know, the one that's resting right there on the arm of the chair you're currently sitting in.

MA – L, S, V

I may be going out on a limb here, but I believe I can with justification claim to be a mature adult. Perhaps it has taken me all of the several decades I've been around to arrive at this point, but here I am. You the reader will have to trust me on this matter, but I'm sure that if you knew me—no, perhaps it's best that you don't know me (and don't go asking any of my friends, either!). Just trust me, and let's proceed.

It is from my perspective as a mature adult that I have come to realize that the TV and movie rating system is not only flawed—it is upside down, bizarro-world, dead wrong. Here's how it works, or purports to work, or just plain doesn't work.

When a program is aired which apparently contains some "objectionable" content (just who is doing the objecting here is perhaps the central point in what is to follow), an advisory system is invoked whereby the viewer-to-be is warned (enticed?) through some alphabetical code *that* this is the case, and *what* is to be found objectionable. Thus a standard warning might read MA – L, S, V. Now the MA is intended to suggest that the upcoming show is to be viewed only by Mature Audiences, while the L, S, V convey, in their turn, that the potentially offending component is the Language used, or the Sex or Violence simulated.

I've been wondering how effective this advisory system is or might be, but the data that might confirm or disconfirm its effectiveness just happens to be non-existent. So if the Movie Gods are free to lay down their laws, unconstrained by any formal evidence, why can't I do likewise? It also occurs to me that while the purported aim of such a ratings system is Protect the Children—let no psychological harm come their way—it is exceedingly doubtful that any ratings committees actually can count, as functioning members, any real honest-to-goodness children. And is this not more than a bit like an all-male congressional committee deciding what should constitute a fair compensation for a woman doing the same job as a man? ("Why, I'd say 77% is more than equitable. Wouldn't you agree, senator?" . . . "Dam generous, 'f y'ask me!") So here, prompted by some real-life observations of actual children and young people, with especially close consideration given to the views, reactions and attitudes of one in particular—*me*—I offer something of a transvaluation of the current cinematic Code of Conduct.

L (anguage)
The paragraph before this last one ended with the word "simulated." I will explain why I chose that word when we take on sex and violence. But let us begin with language, which is what it is, with no simulation required or involved. Whether it is, say, Humphrey Bogart (Sam Spade) letting Brigid O'Shaughnessy know in no uncertain terms "I'm not going to play the sap for you!" (old-speak), or, who knows, some cloistered nun letting loose with a livid string of vulgarities (new-speak), there's no getting around the fact that the words are what they are. So our question here is "to whom might they give offense?"

In answering this I begin with a reminder about the

obvious. The maturity I claim to have earned by being "of a certain age" did not come merely by being that age—let's say (confess to) 70—a nice round number. It comes from being that age, *and from having been and lived through all the ages in between zero and 70.* Yes, I was 8 once, and 13, and 21 and 35 and 50, and I have memories from each era (though the more recent ones are hazier). Nobody starts out old. And being somewhat sensitive to the phenomenon of language, I have observed that it has undergone a considerable evolution over the decades, as the crowd I have associated with has itself evolved. To illustrate what I have in mind here, I suggest we take a brief excursion through that time-honored Shrine of Bad Language: the male locker room.

I have been in and out of locker rooms ever since high school, and have observed how the language that swirls ceilingward amidst the steam has gradually transformed itself. In the early years—high school—there was one overwhelming focus of almost all locker room discourse—girls. Now girls naturally come with certain distinctive attributes, and naturally these attributes figured in much of what was said of them. In fact if we permute a list of those attributes with a similar list of the various acts that one (a boy, of course) did, should, could, or might (if optimal conditions prevailed) perform with, on, or in the presence of said attributes, well, right there you have roughly 85 – 90% of what is commonly recognized as obscenity. And—this is the central point here—all boys (and perhaps all girls, too, though I didn't have the opportunity to hang around in their locker rooms) were right there on the front lines. That is to say, at age 13 (maybe even less if you happened to have a big brother), vulgarity and obscenity are already cherished possessions. *Adolescent boys lay claim to budding manhood in and through their mastery of obscene discourse.*

To be honest, I didn't witness much of a transition in this relationship as I went through college. That was likely the case because I went to an all male college—no, it wasn't a seminary or a military school: just a simple (and very expensive) liberal arts college. And yes, Virginia, there did once exist such institutions, though two years after my graduation the first class of women was admitted, and indeed, the dormitory in which I had spent three years became the first one converted to a women's dorm. (What that conversion involved, I'm not quite sure, beside the removal from the basement of our sacred pool table, upon the hallowed felt of which my sophomore year was laid to shameful waste.) When I lived there, though, the mere presence of a woman—or as we college boys would have said back then, "a girl"—in the first floor lobby could be felt almost immediately in the furthest recesses of the building, as a sort of erotic throb seemed to undulate through the entire structure, rattling windows, knocking pictures out of kilter, torpifying its inhabitants.

The primary topic of discussion in an environment such as this showed little development over that of the high school locker room, though occasionally we would come up for air and maybe talk about sports (which, after all, is why we were in the locker room in the first place). And the language employed therein remained every bit as blue as the atmosphere at Joe Gasser's Bowling Alley on cigar nights. (What am I saying? *Every* night was cigar night at Gasser's!)

As it turned out, my career kept me in college in perpetuity, though eventually I did move to the other end of the classroom, and did most of the talking, where once I only listened (at best; daydreamed or dozed at worst). But I still pursued athletic interests that kept me oriented toward locker rooms, and by now a transformation could be noted—new topics of conversation had sprung up in replacement of the one single one that formerly had dominated. Guys talked about home life, their kids, what the weekend held in store—marriage, it appears, had for the most part bridled those urges that had once run rampant through them and gained feeble fulfillment in . . . mere words. So the stream of vulgarity that once flowed freely was by this time reduced to little more than a trickle—the occasional interjection, often not even that.

Now in my later years (and with many of the guys in my current locker room situation being similarly "well-seasoned"), I can report, with no small degree of amusement, that the principal topic of conversation has noticeably shifted. Girls, women seem but a distant dream—a green flash on the horizon: "Look—there goes the sun; now here comes the flash; watch for it! Oops, not today!" The new obsession is—oh, I know, blame it on La Jolla—*money*. Hardly a verbal exchange can be heard which does not set out from, revolve around, or at least make some salient reference to a dollar figure. Even the fellow who jabbers on incessantly into his phone in some unknown language still peppers his discourse with frequent appeals to the verbal unit "meel-yun." (And I guess he'd better keep peppering it so, just to be able to maintain the payments on that Maserati sport convertible he drives!) And unless you find obscenity in money (perhaps some do: "obscene wealth"?), the atmosphere has cleansed itself of anything "objectionable."

I cannot think of a single film that earned itself an R rating based solely on frequent references to money. (*The Wolf of Wall Street* doesn't qualify here, as it is not the money talk that offended many moviegoers, but the proliferation of F-bombs that laid waste the verbal landscape.)

The conclusion I draw from the above considerations? That the Urge to Obscenity varies inversely with one's level of maturity.

But this has been my personal journey through time. How about those tender adolescents I started out with (one of which I started out as)? What can we say of the current state of affairs as regards their propensity toward obscenity? Well, having fallen in step behind a knot of them a while back, I am happy to report that not only have they sustained the noble tradition—they have enriched it with linguistic sallies that left even me in wonderment. How the term "cluster," for example, could be applied to anything but groups of stars or arrangements of jewels left my head spinning, but there it was in all clarity, for them to know and for me to figure out.

Give it a try yourself sometime, if you have children of the appropriate age around the house. Oh, I'm not inviting you to eavesdrop on them—well, come to think of it I *am* inviting you to do *just that*. See if you don't hear things that show the willingness of today's youth "to (sic) boldly go where no one has gone before," into the tantalizingly murky recesses of vulgarity. Then ask yourself "How often do I feel inclined to go there myself anymore?" Not so much, I suspect.

My overall conclusion is, therefore, that the label MA-L should be read as suggesting: *"mature audiences are likely to be offended by some of the language in the following production."*

Or, more succinctly, *"ADOLESCENTS ONLY!"*

S (ex) & V (iolence)
As I suggested in the above section, language is what it is—what you hear is, well, what you hear. Oh, maybe there are layers of symbolism concealed behind any dialogue, but there is still nothing "fake" about the language you do hear. In the realms of cinematic sex and violence, however, there is a lot of fakery; in fact barring accident or incident it's *all* fake.

I suppose an actor may derive a bit of titillation from an erotic scene, but I suspect it would be *very* little—probably less than might be enjoyed by various members of the team of camera operators, sound specialists, script consultants, make-up artists, drama coaches, and whoever else might just happen to pass by or be stationed on the set at the time of filming. But even if a performer should get a little zing from a scene simulating some sexual activity, nothing of a *violent* nature ever occurs on camera—at least nothing that ever reaches the screen—the actors' lawyers simply wouldn't allow it! I recall once passing some time in a laundromat many years back, and leafing through one of the only magazines available there—what else? *People*—in which I came across an article about a 70s matinee idol, one Jan-Michael Vincent (where is he now?!). In it he described himself (yes, that's right) as a "high risk danger man"(!), which led me to wonder, what risks did he really run? Well, as I read on, I learned that the director of the film under discussion, Sam Peckinpah, was an extremely *demanding* director, who *forced* certain actors to repeat a running scene, so that by day's end poor Jan-Michael had *blisters* on his feet. Oh, *the humanity*! No doubt the occasional stunt man or woman does suffer an injury; over the decades, in fact, a couple have died. But so far as the film is concerned, these unhappy events are left lying on the cutting room floor.

The question I'm posing here, then, is: Who is more likely to be negatively influenced by viewing a cinematic simulation of something sexual or violent? Our movie ratings committee believes it to be the younger viewers. I have my doubts about that. For evidence to support this bit of skepticism, I retreat into my own past—I was young once, remember.

I recall once, an age and a half ago, accompanying my father to a film which proved to be a massive bore. Why he took me at all is puzzling to me now, and was probably puzzling to me then, although I suspect that children are puzzled by the curious behavior of adults so often that they learn to live through it without questions, without harm (similar, perhaps, to the way the desert dwellers take the searing sun for granted, and simply protect themselves accordingly. But they don't seem to raise the question "Why do we have to put up with this *heat*? Why don't we just move to the seashore?)

I was nine at the time. I know that because I looked it up on Google. No, Google hasn't become that intrusive and specific—at least not *yet*: it gave the date of the release of the film as 1953. The film in question was *Niagara*, and it starred Marilyn Monroe. *Marilyn Monroe!* Apparently, though not her first film, it was her break-out film. So it's easy to see why my father was keen to go and have a look, but for me it was an afternoon most tediously spent. I mean, there was nothing to *see*! No cowboys; no Indians; no sea battles, no dogfights overhead; no swashbuckling pirates—not even a wicked witch. Just Marilyn Monroe. I would have preferred Yosemite Sam! In truth, exactly half a century elapsed before I was again to be as bored in a movie theater as I was in that one, this next time coming that fateful evening in 2003 when it took all the power of will I had in me to maintain a semblance of consciousness during *Lost in Translation*.

Yet Marilyn was Marilyn, and no doubt her mere presence quickened the imaginations of millions of men. But she worked no magic on that nine-year-old boy. So if I were to rate a movie such as that, I would declare it harmless for the under-13 set, but hazardous to the emotional stability of a grown man.

By contrast, I am inclined to assign an MA-S rating to *Casablanca*. Honestly, what could an eleven-year-old comprehend of the complicated triangle formed by Rick, Ilsa, and Victor, which forms the centerpiece of the whole film? And he wouldn't even be left to wonder just what or how much transpired between Rick and Ilsa on that last night, which proved to be the eve of the next day's foggy departure. Same thing holds for *Gone With the Wind*—definitely fit for the MA-S label. Act One—the phase before the intermission—ends with Rhett sweeping Scarlett off her feet and hauling her up that huge stairway. Then Act Two—when we return, popcorn-laden, from the intermission—begins with Rhett and Scarlett playing joyously with some little girl. *Like where did* she *come from?!* Did she maybe just show up at their door one morning?! Did I miss something while I was in line back at the concession stand?

As to violence, both the kid in me and the kids out there speak out against being excluded from every such spectacle. It is the adult in me, however, who currently holds sway, and who will have nothing of what Hollywood offers up on this score.

I believe your average ten-year-old, by the time he is called down to breakfast on any given school-day morning, will already have obliterated scores of baddies of all types and persuasions, be they terrestrial or extra-terrestrial. We're only talking simulation, remember—simulation is all Hollywood has to offer—and the swarm of video games that so captivate the younger set are remarkable both in their degree of realistic depiction and the extent of the violence depicted.

Not wishing to become annoyingly analytic here—it won't last more than a couple sentences, I promise!—but I suspect that certain elements of, shall we say, civilized behavior develop over time, and in the case of a ten-year-old (I'm giving or taking a couple years here—remember, I have no lab work to back me up, but neither do my antagonists, the Lawgivers of Hollywood), it just seems that the dual capacities of empathy and sympathy might not have developed yet to their full extent. Empathy I see as a psychological attainment—the ability "to feel as another is feeling"—while sympathy is a moral quality, one that still involves feeling, but which may involve, say, feeling the need to provide aid, or to offer comfort, but not necessarily duplicating the feeling-state of another person. (Of course a great many "adults" seem not to have undergone this "growth spurt" either; a simple test: look in their wallets and you are likely to find their NRA membership card tucked in there somewhere.) There may well be developmental reasons responsible for in some sense anesthetizing younger folks from the full range of moral experience. That at least is the hypothesis I'm floating here. Now back to an area I am more directly and comfortably conversant with... *me*.

As a kid I was enamored of Indian-slaying cowboy films. I had my own cowboy gear, complete with a pair of six-shooters (picture available on request), and though merely toys (they may have been cap pistols), they were nevertheless made of metal—I can still smell and in a strange way taste the metal. Why, one suspicious look back then from one of today's shoot-first policemen and I might well not be around to write this!

A good war movie likewise captured and held my interest. The time frame I speak of was actually only a few years after the close of WW II, and Hollywood was still celebrating the victory (which is looking now like the last victory we are ever going be able to celebrate, unless you count that magnificent triumph over those frightful Cuban airport workers in Granada). Airplanes—bombers, fighter planes—in particular fed my youthful imagination. So naturally when a movie came to town that celebrated one of the virtual founders of our modern day air force, Billy Mitchell, I was more than happy to be taken to see that one. This time even my mother came along! And why not: the central role belonged not to some twenty-something blonde bombshell, but to Gary Cooper.

But alas, this turned out badly for me, as well, though it was not boredom that I suffered from this time but disappointment, frustration, irritation. Here I went to see German warships blown to oblivion, and yet the film hardly strayed beyond courtroom walls. I was eleven—how did I know what I should expect from *The* **Court Martial** *of Billy Mitchell*?! Had I but known at that time what the term "oxymoronic" signified, I would without any doubt have aimed that particular pejoration squarely at the notion of "courtroom drama." Once again the adult world had led me astray. What strange interests did they manifest!

It was this adult world, after all, that found something objectionable in the classic Road Runner / Wily Coyote cartoons that we kids took such delight in. Somehow they disapproved of the way Coyote would successively flatten, immolate or simply blow himself to bits in futile pursuit of that snarky Road Runner. We didn't even ask how he managed to reassemble himself for his next assault. We just laughed. But they censored this silliness out of existence.

I did finally undergo the "growth spurt" that led me from childhood savagery to adult civility (though I still retain an affection for the Road Runner cartoons—*cartoon* violence? *Seriously*?!). I graduated from war lover to militant pacifist, would not dream of having a six-shooter, or any other kind of shooter around the house, and am now positively repulsed by depictions of violence of any sort. Even watching football can at times be a challenge, and speak but the name Quentin Tarantino and I recoil with a shudder. So once again, MA-V: "suitable only for adult viewing" has come to suggest, to the adult me, "to be avoided at all costs"!

Let the children have their fill of all the violence Hollywood can send their way. That is all behind me now, and so it must be. Life is short and youth is shorter yet.

Deo gratias.

DEAR GLORIA

[*Here follows a reply I made to a local columnist, on the occasion of her tragic announcement that she finally purchased an iPhone.*]

Hello Gloria,

Clearly your techno-incompetence is in no league with mine. Case in point—you *actually* own a cell phone! Why, it was only a couple years ago that, due to a kitchen remodel and the subsequent need to do away with all those phone wires lacing certain of the old cabinets like cobwebs, we installed a *cordless* unit. But still when it rings and I go answer it, I hover in the vicinity of the rack on which it sits, as if I were held there by some invisible wire. Oh, I admit, once in a while it occurs to me to go sit in the living room and talk, but usually the calls I receive are solicitations for donations to one noble cause or another, so the conversation ends before I have any need to "get comfortable." In fact since talking on the phone has never been a strong suit of mine—we might say I am phonophobic, if a bit of neologizing is allowed—one of the few pleasures I derive from driving a car resides in knowing that as long as I'm in it, nobody will be calling me. This too seems to pit me against the tide of contemporary society, the great majority of whom take their need for idle conversation right onto the highway with them, often at great risk to themselves and their fellow travelers.

And surely I will never be embarrassed at a concert by an inopportune ringing emanating from my jacket pocket, as happened recently, I'm sure you read, to a gentleman in the audience of the New York Philharmonic, whose calypso-laced ring tone sounded out just as a Mahler symphony was drawing to its lugubrious, self-pitying ("Why did she have to leave me for that inferior Gropius creature?!") close. Perhaps if Mahler himself had been present for that event, he might have perked up and thought, "Why didn't I think of that?! Why all this gloom?! I want to *live! **Live!!***"

But if you are indeed inept at handling yours, you might consider leaving it home when you head off to the concert hall.

Further evidence to your techno-aptitude, however: *you know what an APP actually is,* and you know—though I'll just have to trust you on this—that such "things" can actually be purchased in stores (only "things" are sold in stores, aren't they?). Granted the fictitious one you were describing is not likely to be found, still it shows that you at least dwell in the *suburbs* of Technoville. I recently asked a friend what an APP was, but I don't recall getting an answer—he just shook his head and chuckled.

Far be it from me to boast, but if you can gleefully think of yourself as Pleistocene, I would have to be Primal Ooze.

To add a bit more support to this claim, I can point out that I still own and use—are you ready for this?—a *camera*. And in a dim room I actually open it up and introduce into its innards . . . *film*! And when I use it I adjust the shutter speed, focus the lens and look at the subject through the view-finder. Nowadays it seems people hold their photographic apparati strangely aloft, as if using them to shield their eyes from the sun, then suddenly a click can be heard, and they ask you over to show you what they just photographed, with no mediation by any drugstore clerk, no one-hour wait. But like Cardinal Bellarmine when invited by Galileo to view the heavens through that new-fangled, sin-laden contraption he was calling a telescope, I staunchly resolve to decline their invitation, out of a similar fear that to accede to their request might leave in tatters my entire *weltanschauung*.

Oh, and neither of my cars talks to me. My roadway guidance system is provided entirely by my Thomas Brothers map. I *have*, however, on my regular walks in our neighborhood, provided the correct directions to dozens of passing motorists who, in a nearby location, are mysteriously and systematically led astray from their designated target—a local monument with a wrap-around view—by their beloved, sweet-voiced GPS, who inscrutably advises them to take a left turn a scant fifty yards and one bend in the road before they would have reached their proposed destination.

In a word, the cure for techno-depression suggested to you by your younger son is not techno-skill. No, he is dead wrong: the true and genuine cure lies in the self-affirmation that results in—or emerges from—*techno-scorn*. Or if you are a more sanguine type of individual, techno-*pity*—pity for those lost souls, mesmerized by their little hand-held devices, led they know not where like the pod people whose bodies had been snatched and their wills wholly given over to some mysterious Outside Power. (When that film first came out in the fifties, it was thought that the alleged power might be the Communists. If a second remake comes out any time soon, that power might be taken to represent the Koch brothers.) See them in any mall, circulating about the Apple Shop, awaiting, like fearful penitents, the next technological nudge that will make their little lives a little bit less little. And all the while, alongside them, almost touching them but still unseen for the blinding glare imposed by that demonic iPhone, there passes a *real* world with *real* people in it, and real beauties to apprehend and absorb.

No—I won't surrender my land line until they pry it from my cold ... *dead* ... **hand!**

KNOWLEDGE IS ... BORING

I recently indulged in a little game that my friends and I would commonly play with one another, back in the day—kind of an on-the-spot film trivia challenge. I asked someone if they could identify who uttered the line "Rotten kids! You work your *life* out!!" and in what movie. (It's hard to come up with an answer to either of those questions, of course, without the other tagging along immediately.)

No sooner had I offered the challenge, though, than I realized that, rather than lighting the fuse to a brain teaser, I would in all likelihood be presented with the correct answer in probably 6.7 seconds or less.

Used to be you would puzzle over things like that, dig around in the recesses of your brain, say the line over and over to yourself until it started to concretize in your mind, and an image would start to take shape in your imagination. At a certain point you might stop *saying* the line and begin *growling* it—maybe even grabbing a piece of paper and tearing it in half and in half again as you blurted out in triumph "Lee J. Cobb . . . *Twelve Angry Men*!!"

Not now, though. Now you just head straight to the Google bar, type in the line, and there it is, right at the top of the page: "12 Angry Men – wikiquote."

Once upon a time we would have sifted through our memory, as we might go rooting about in the attic for several hours in search of that old high school yearbook we just had to get another look at, to remind ourselves how

Harvey Polishuk combed his hair back then, or what Jackie Kloby looked like. When at long last we laid hands on it, we would give out a yelp of recognition, blow the dust off it, and plunge into its pages one more time. Now it's as if it had been lying right there on the kitchen table, the length of an arm away all along. For years!

We guys used to entertain ourselves back in the dorm with Rock & Roll quizzes (this obviously bespeaks an era prior to co-ed dorms; in fact it was at a college that hadn't yet even gone co-ed!): What was the biggest hit of Dicky Doo and the Don'ts (probably their only hit)? Who did "In the still . . . show doapum showbie doh . . . of the nieeight . . .?" And what *was* Little Richard really saying?! It sounded like "Lucille . . . you doan do you ku ku kweel," but that couldn't be (unless, as a man of the cloth, he had fallen into some sort of *raptus*, and was singing in tongues). So we'd puzzle away, try out various possibilities—my roommate suggested it was "You don't do your sister's will," but that seemed silly to me—how do you get "sister" out of "ku ku"?!

And on we would go, until something sprang up to wrest our attention away from such critical questions as these, and direct our considerable mental energy down more fruitful paths, like preparing for tomorrow's exam. Or we would simply have to admit defeat and, for want of any determinate mode of adjudication, surrender. Well, folks, I regret to admit it, but that was then and this is now and my roommate was right: I just googled "Lucille – lyrics" and sure enough, there it is, "You don't do your sister's will." And speaking of "Google," back at the time being spoken of the only Google anyone was conversant about was a cartoon character named Barney Google, noted for his "goo- goo- googly eyes," and for having "a wife that was three times his size," or so the song about him informed us (feel free to check my memory here, but I think I'll just let this one lie). Come to think about it, it makes for a rather odd eponym for the most astonishing search engine yet invented, no? (And yes, there was actually a song in those days about a cartoon character, a light-hearted song about a goofy character. Nowadays the only cartoon character who might be celebrated in song would have to be endowed with super powers, or be some kind of relentless killing machine. Back then, it seems, we could live in harmony with the simply goofy.)

How disappointing this all is! Where once one of us would have come up with the answer, accompanying it with that sly, knowing smirk that said "I got it, man, I just *got* it!" now someone whips out one of those little phone thingeys, and straightaway comes up with the answer. They still might well give off a sly, knowing smirk, but it would be prompted not by their deep-pocketed memory, but by their digital dexterity—how with feather fingers they dance the tiny screen this way and that in the manner that their Lord and Master Steve Jobs, to whom they owe full obeisance, would have them do.

In fact memory is becoming increasingly expendable. If you can remember what pocket you store that little device in, and how to go about feeding it a question, that is about all you need in the way of memory anymore.

I was in a reading room in the Athenaeum the other day—a delightful little art and music library, endowed many decades ago by Ellen Browning Scripps, which is situated here in the heart of the village of La Jolla. The room is filled with lovely tomes, through the aid of which you could inform yourself about almost anything that had anything to do with things artistic. How delightful it once was to pore through those volumes in search of whatever it was you were in search of; and what other delicacies might you discover in your search! Now you can save yourself a trip downtown: just type, say, "Fra Angelica" onto your Google bar, and read away at any of the 1,030,000 citations that your little gadget just presented you with in .34 of a second. Wherever you might be. (*Ready? Set? Go!*)

Used to be a scholar would make complicated arrangements in order to spend a summer, or a semester, or a year, in, say, Paris, camped out daily in the *Bibliothêque Nationale*, or the *Bibliothêque de la Sorbonne*, to carry out research on books many of which were available there and only there. Of course you would step out to the nearest bistro for lunch; and the nights were all your own (hoo hah!), and all the while you were right there, in the City of Lights. Now I suspect that, with university and governmental budgets tightening all across the country and the world, expeditions of this sort are more and more frequently being carried out in the (ho hum) comfort of one's own study, which I'll just bet doesn't have a domed ceiling that reaches to a height of about 50', and whose surrounding walls are lined with centuries-old books.

I guess Yogi was right—nostalgia isn't what it used to be.

Oops!—turns out that wasn't Yogi: I have just been informed, via Google, that it was Simone Signoret--the title of her autobiography, in fact. But where did she come up with such a title. (Could she maybe have been a Yogi fan, or at least a Yankee fan?) And what would its French equivalent be? Let's see now, what if I were to Google . . . ?

THE LAST HURRAH (An American Tragedy?)

I was 62 years old and I had just been bitten on the head by a fellow about one-third my age. As I stood sponging the blood away from my eyes, I finally asked myself the question that any sane person would have asked twenty years earlier—and straightaway received a negative response!—is it really worth it?

The head bite occurred during a pick-up basketball game down at the local playground. I had just secured a rebound when the aforementioned individual, who seemed to question whether the ball was as securely in my possession as I believed it to be, took it upon himself to attempt to wrest it away from my grasp. What choice had I but to introduce, with all due politeness, his teeth to the top of my head?

If blame in this incident is to be weighed and distributed, the heaviest share of it should be laid at the feet of Bill Dougherty. He was the basketball coach back at Toms River High School who year after year failed to acknowledge my obvious superiority at the game. Each year the tryouts would roll around; each year at the end of the second day I would check the list of boys who had made it through the cut; and each year I would fail to find my name on that list. A little respect showed at a critical age can last a lifetime.

Respect denied, however, also lasts a lifetime—it haunts one to his final days: recall Charles Foster Kane's "Rosebud"; and it has been suggested that if Hitler's art teacher had complimented him on his painting, well, someone else would have had to step forward and claim the title of Bloodthirsty Demon of the Twentieth Century.

But if you haven't guessed, I offered this last paragraph tongue-in-cheekedly. Mr. Dougherty was 100% justified in cutting me, as I was light years away from knowing, or even being capable of learning how to integrate successfully into a team. Still, I refused to stop playing, trying. There was always a game *somewhere*, and I finally did work my way—in my thirties!—into a group that could and eventually did educate me on the fine points of teamwork. I found my way to them after I had become a professor at the University of Kentucky, which is quite a good place to be situated if you burn to learn about the game of basketball. Most of those in the group were very talented (one was—still is, in fact—in the NBA Hall of Fame), and they succeeded in making my inadequacies crystal clear to me, and over time led me to see what I should have been doing all along. Actually there's a lot of abuse politely concealed in these latter two clauses, for it was, to them, a labor of hate, and they took it on vigorously—*venomously*! To many of them—a critical mass of them, it seemed—I carried with me the stigma not only of being unschooled in the game, but of being (*ugh!*) a *yankee*. Still I vowed to persist, endure, and *learn*, and by the time I was, say, 44, I felt I had indeed learned how best to lend whatever talents I possessed (or by that time, what few were left to me) to a total team effort, the only acceptable outcome of which was winning (as opposed, previously, to looking good, regardless of how things turned out). Of course this came rather too late to impress the other kids—or the coach!--back at Toms River High, but better late than never.

To return to the matter at hand, I was, you'll remember, bleeding from the scalp, so I decided to call it a day and return home to ice down the gash. Home was perhaps not the most welcoming environment in these circumstances, as my wife had often enunciated a simple rule of conduct for me to follow: If you get injured, don't come home. I always took that to be more of an invitation to prudence, rather than some heartless prohibition—and sure enough I was permitted reentry, though not without a dose of sarcasm that rivaled in temperature the ice pack I had placed on my head. It was thus within this welter of actual pain and feigned domestic distress that I set about to wondering whether maybe she was right after all, and I should bring this "career" that had begun in the backyards of various friends a half century earlier, adjacent to the other ocean, to a semi-dignified close.

By coincidence—and if it weren't for coincidences there would be no tales to tell, isn't that right?—I was speaking a couple days later with a neighbor, a former player himself with USC (perhaps the conversation was touched off by the bandage on my head), and he wondered if I had heard of a Senior Olympics League (that's pretty close, at least, to the name he mentioned). It's a statewide basketball league for players 55 years old and above, with local chapters in any cities, towns or neighborhoods where a quorum of such individuals feels inclined to get together and play. They even have playoffs and crown a statewide champion each year. My neighbor brought it up figuring that in an environment such as that I was much less likely to get bitten or otherwise assaulted than on any local playground open to all comers. I could only concur with his judgment, so with very little weighing of pros and cons (after all, what could possibly go wrong?), I resolved to give it a shot, asked him where and when to present myself, and set about to readying myself for a new adventure on the hardwood.

A few days later there I was at the Y, standing on the sidelines, waiting to take the court after the game in progress terminated. I talked a bit with a few of the others who waited with me, starting out by asking whether I was in the right place, such as my neighbor had described it. "Well, you *do* have to be at least 55 to join in," I was admonished. Did I really look so young that my age might be an issue?! True, I still weighed the same as I did when I was 17, but I handily met most of the other criteria of organic deterioration. But imagine—getting carded at 62! I assured them that I fell comfortably above their required age limit.

Finally the game we had been watching ended, and a new group that included me headed toward the basket to take a few warm-up shots. The framework was 3-on-3, half court—the essence of basketball, with all that superfluous running from one end to the other strained out, leaving only passing, cutting, screening, shooting. As we divided into teams one of my new-found teammates informed me of his physical situation, to wit: "I have a pacemaker and an artificial hip." "Oh *baby*!" I gloated inwardly, "One last chance to *dom-min-nate*!"

Since I appeared, well, suspiciously young, I was assigned the responsibility of guarding the "star" of the other team. "He can shoot the lights out," one fellow told me, and indeed while we were warming up I did observe that he had a very nice touch. The ex-NBAer I used to play with back in Kentucky was able, given one minute of observation, to discern all the important strengths and weaknesses a potential opponent possessed, and adjust his own game accordingly. Fancying I had absorbed some of his methodology, I positively relished the defensive assignment!

Play started up top, with the ball in the hands of this "star." I gave him a respectful space to work in, and he quickly put up a shot. One nothing, favor them. Now the reason one gives a shooter a bit of room when you are at some distance from the basket stems from the fear that if you move in too close to him he might, with one quick spin or feint-and-step, be around you, with a clear path to the basket in front of him. So here I pose to you the reader a question: Just how many times do you think a sixty-something man can quick around a defender and explode to the basket for a layup? The correct answer, I suggest, is "somewhere between 'zero' and 'one'." Should he actually pull it off once, expect to watch him lapse into hyperventilation for the next ten minutes or so, while you have your way with him.

Armed with this bit of insight, I proceeded to close up on him as tightly as I could, to force him to work hard for every shot, or, what for him must have been worse yet, to pass to a teammate and let him have a try at it. I was so successful with this tactic that after a few minutes of it he simply laid his wrist against my chest and pushed, causing me to stagger back a couple steps. Even if you don't know much about the game of basketball, you can still tell that is illegal. But for me, there, on that day, it was cause for pure delight, because it told me *"I have arrived!"* And we were still just half way through my first game.

From being "carded," to receiving the critical defensive

assignment, to the prospect of being able to dominate a game, to the rapid validation of my defensive efforts—this was a heady concoction indeed: The rebirth of an athletic career in the same month that I received my first social security check!

Hardly had ten minutes elapsed after that rewarding shove to my sternum when I scored on a simple put-back, in close. The winning basket, capping off the glorious latter-day rebirth of a nearly defunct career? Hardly. Contrary to the flow this narrative seems to have been following up to this point, I have to confess that I have no accurate recollection as to which side actually did win that game. At this point, the toss of a coin would be as reliable an indicator as my own memory. The only significance that basket held for me, then and forevermore, was that it was the last one I would ever score in a competitive endeavor. I knew as much at that very moment, because it was accompanied with such pain that I questioned whether it was worth the trouble, just to put one point on an imaginary scoreboard. For, a few minutes earlier, I had fallen and broken my wrist—my *left* wrist: the wrist I shot, dribbled, and for that matter wrote and ate with.

How such an injury happened was a blur then which hasn't clarified itself any over the ensuing years. The only clear aspect of it that remains is that I committed the grave error (one that I had preached against to others on several occasions) of breaking my fall with my hand, and not absorbing the impact by rolling onto my shoulder. Beyond that I have a vague sense that I and someone else were crossing in front of each other—"Is this a leg I see before me" asked my inner Macbeth, "the ankle in my path?" Such was my impression, and yet my on-the-spot instinctive calculation suggested that it would be out of the way by the time I got there.

Certainly it would have been with the players of my earlier association, back in Kentucky. In that venue, serious athletes often joined in, young men with young bodies and NBA credentials to go with them. And I used to marvel how certain of them were able to set themselves in motion far away from the basket, and yet with just a couple dribbles and a few steps they would suddenly be hovering over the rim preparing to throw the ball down through it. (One of my greatest defensive efforts came against one such individual—James Lee, a massive star on Kentucky's 1978 national championship team. As he charged down the floor in preparation for one of his thunderous dunks, I left the floor with him, as if to contest his shot. He found my presumptuousness so amusing that he burst out laughing in mid air, lost the handle of the ball, and fumbled it away harmlessly.) Players like him seemed almost able to squeeze distance together as one might an accordion—do we perhaps have here some proof of Einstein's radical revision of the space-time continuum, in which space itself is deemed capable of bending, stretching, *contracting*?!

Well, suffice it to say that the gentlemen with whom I was playing on this fateful day offered no such confirmation of the Einsteinian model of the universe. The spatial framework within which they moved about was strictly old-world, Newtonian, and their movements were readily measurable by the crudest of eighteenth-century instruments. My mind, alas, was apparently cruder yet in forming its estimates, in calculating that a certain leg would have been out of my path by the time I reached where it had been. For it turned out that it was still there, and down

I went.

"If you get injured, don't bother to come home"—remember that little epigram? I certainly did. Naturally when a genuine injury actually did come to pass, she was much more sympathetic: "Maybe it's not broken; only sprained." I smiled a weak smile: "Maybe." But I had sprained enough joints over the years to know that this was something else. In any case I didn't go directly home. First there was a visit to the ER at the hospital, followed by X-rays, the fitting of a temporary cast, (preceded by the cutting off of a wedding ring that hadn't left its resident finger for decades—but that finger was now swelling fast!), and the scheduling of surgery in the coming days to pin the bones together again. Only after all that could I return to the house, where I would spend the next six weeks as the type of indolent burden I had hoped never to become.

And this, dear reader, is where the flow of ideas seems invariably to lead me. I cast this way and that in search of an upbeat ending—"you leave 'em laughing when you go"—but if there is one, I systematically miss the turn to it. Each rereading, carried out in hope that some bright flash would show me the way, leaves me instead disconsolate. I am reminded by this of an interview I once heard with the great Italian/Swiss sculptor Alberto Giacometti. In it he was explaining, almost apologetically, why the busts he was sculpting of his (beloved) brother Diego seemed invariably to take the shape of Freddie Kruger's unsightly fraternal twin, on his last visit to Guantanamo. "I can't help it; it's just the way my hands capture what my eye sees." And thus he captured for us in words something of the weakness of creative power: no mere worldly wish can override the raw power of the creative impulse. Now if an artist of the immense skill of *a Giacometti still cannot find a way to make his brother's effigy look respectable—or even human!—what hope have I (little me) of diverting the direction this topic has imposed on me? But do read on. Maybe the next piece will help.*

WITH ANY LUCK

🐧

To get things started, what would you say the following three individuals (defined here entirely in terms of their professions) have in common: a dentist, an electrician, and an optometrist? Let's see, only two are in the medical profession. Two—the electrician and the optometrist—deal with things that go in, or are found in *sockets*. The dentist and the electrician of course both charge *waaaaay* too much for their services. No, we're not even warm here. What binds them all together is that in recent weeks each one had occasion to preface a salient comment to me with the words "With any luck . . ." Well, OK, in one case I had to supply the phrase myself, because the speaker caught himself in time, leaving a verbal vacuum begging to be filled in. And since it was obvious just what was dangling tantalizingly before his mind's eye, I simply spared him the trouble, and any accompanying embarrassment, by snatching it away before he could chomp down on it.

First came the dentist. In a routine visit, he detected in an X-ray some form of decay down beneath a tooth, seemingly (to me) out of reach of any treatment short of actually removing the tooth. He gave a name to this problem which I now forget, but even before forgetting it I couldn't find it either in my (allegedly) unabridged dictionary, or in the Dictionary of the Gods—the internet. Since it was a tooth he had previously worked on, I was (and am) wondering if he didn't just invent the term as a shield for some procedural misstep he might have committed. Time, or perhaps a more inclusive dictionary, will tell.

Incidentally, this does pose, for me, a larger problem than just some dental work and the discomfort and expense that such an ordeal would involve. There is a question of pride at issue here—a pride, indeed, that could extend *for centuries*! For I have made it this far through life (which, if you haven't yet guessed you will soon, is pretty far) with a full set of the divinely prescribed number of teeth, and I should very much like to take that set to the grave with me. Why, this might prove to be the greatest, most singular achievement of my entire life! I can even see boasting of it in an epitaph carved on my tombstone, thusly:

STILL GOT ALL 32
HOW ABOUT YOU?

But there's no need to get ahead of ourselves here.

In any case the dentist may have sensed my plight, as he quickly chimed in that he had had patients with this same issue who went maybe five years before requiring active treatment of it, "so maybe, with any luck . . . " and as he paused I filled in the rest myself with a pacifying chuckle: "I'll be dead."

Yes, that was indeed the lucky break he was aiming at, but was too nice to utter.

Moving right along (as Kermit the Frog used to say), it wasn't long after that experience that I checked in with the optometrist to see if anything could be done to clear up my visual field some. In recent years, with a proliferation of floaters and a series of what they call PVDs (to spare themselves the trouble of pronouncing and explaining "Posterior Vitreous Detachment" to an unsuspecting and unprepared patient), I sometimes seem to be viewing the world as through a fish tank, darkly, with little black guppies darting this way and that, and diaphanous ferns gently oscillating in the artificial current.

It turns out I will have to accept and perhaps even come to enjoy this spectacle, as none of it is reversible or curable. (Medical researchers seem only to work on cures for the real bad stuff, but in the realm of ocular maladies, PVDs and floaters are somewhat on the order of the common cold.) In giving my eyes a thorough looking over, the only treatable problems the doctor did detect were nascent cataracts in both eyes. Their existence had actually been pointed out to me by another doctor maybe five years earlier, who started angling for a surgical treatment within the year. The present doctor, though, did his best to downplay any need for surgery in the near future, and "his best" was maybe a bit too good, as it terminated with the words "so, with any luck . . . " followed by a knowing chuckle that I willingly joined in on, having only recently "been there, done that." It seemed we were starting to home in on a convenient resolution to many a problem. Oh, and just by the way, I'm betting that the doctor of five years earlier owns a substantially bigger boat than this nicer but more (brutally) honest one does.

This brings us to the electrician.

We gave up some square footage when we moved to our current home, but made up for it and then some in cubic footage, with ceilings that rise to 17 1/2 feet at the apex. Since we are in a warm climate area, the heat loss such ceilings produce is a negligible factor. We have no complaints on any score, in fact, but for this one: the builder saw fit to imbed a spotlight in the ceiling just below the apex. And lights do burn out.

This prompted the age old question—don't tell me you've never posed it yourself!—"How does the average person with maybe a 7-foot ladder, unscrew and replace a light bulb that is 16 feet off the floor?" Well, in fact there do exist devices that have been created just for that purpose—extendable shafts with a variety of "seizing" elements that can be attached to the end: suction cups, claws and the like. The suction cup, though often efficacious (surprisingly so) at more reasonable heights, plainly lost its efficacy at 16 feet. So next I tried the gripper. Using it I did manage to pull the light free, but in doing so I brought the entire canister with it! And there it all dangled, seemingly precariously--though what could cause it to fall, as there seemed to be no "gravitational supplements" available at such a height? Figuring, therefore, that I had done *my* part, in succeeding to destroy the whole apparatus, the time had come to call on an electrician to resolve the problem.

A couple months later he showed up (really!). He surveyed the situation, in so doing taking into account, apparently, not merely the inaccessibility of the light fixture but the look and age of the person (me) who had dislodged the canister in the first place, and recommended that the current incandescent light be replaced by one of the LED variety. Though more expensive up front, they are reputed to last way longer than any of the old fashioned lights. "That way," he judged, *"with any luck"* (pregnant pause giving way to smirk), "you will have moved somewhere else by the time the LED gives out."

So there we are. Who will be next to join in the fun fest? The Banker?—"That's quite a considerable outstanding balance on your mortgage, but with any luck . . ." The Auto Mechanic?—"Your PT Cruiser should be good for another 50,000 miles, and given the amount you drive it, who knows, with any luck . . ."

I'm still not settled on the precise formulation of that dental-themed epitaph, by the way, so if you the reader can think of any way to sharpen it up, feel free to contact me with your recommended alternative. Who knows, I may still be around to receive it. With any luck.

THE END OF SEX
(AS WE KNEW IT)

Once upon a time—and it was a pretty long time, in fact, including the first 40 years or so of my life plus an indeterminate number of centuries before that—people were not afraid to use the word "sex" to distinguish between the male and the female of any species that permitted of such a distinction (anemones, jellyfish, and other such ambiguous creatures were excused, but it readily applied to the rest of us). It took no special boldness for a woman to assert "I do not know one of my sex; no woman's face remember, save, from my glass, mine own . . . ." The woman in this case happened to be Miranda, bantering with Antonio in *The Tempest*—now that takes us back 400 years right there.

But should some demure modern-day Miranda have a mind to express such a thought in the current vernacular, she would without a doubt declare (gravely abusing the metric scheme in the process): "I do not know one of my *gender*, . . . " as if being "of a sex" was cause to blush, or whether it might give some modern-day Antonio second thoughts about whether this really was the woman for him. What has happened to us, that whenever possible we shy away from any mention of sex, in favor of the more insipid and, well, sexless "gender"?

"Gender" seemed, at least since Elizabethan times, to

be an exclusively grammatical term. As such, an *adjective*, say, might be said to agree with a *noun* in number (singular, plural) and *gender* (masculine, feminine). But adjectives weren't—and so far as I know, still aren't—biological organisms of any sort. Nor are nouns, even in heavily "gendered" languages such as French, where "table," "war," and "torture" are *feminine*, and "duty," "fire," and "femur" are *masculine*. So when and how, exactly, did "sex" come to collapse into "gender"?

I suspect the transition began maybe a generation ago. That was the time when Feminism was firmly establishing itself in the academic sector as a respectable wing in the larger sociological-philosophical edifice. It appears that then and there the term was borrowed from the grammatical realm in order to underscore differences between men and women that reached beyond simple biology. This seemed a perfectly legitimate act of borrowing: language, after all, is forever in flux, so why not rescue a term from the tedious realm of grammar (a realm in which fewer and fewer people can find their way about anyway), and endow it with a new identity, a new life—witness protection *for a noun!*? *Gender* was thus adopted as a means of highlighting differences between men and women in social, professional, domestic, and personal contexts—the demands and expectations placed on each; the set of roles each was expected to play. These seemed to be differences that the simple mention of sex, and its straightforward connection to biology, did not adequately cover. No problem so far. Score one for the Feminists.

I started to detect a problem a while back when I was called upon to fill out a form on which I was asked to indicate my *gender*. The form did at least provide an M and an

F, so it was still obvious which letter one should circle, even though, on *my* reading, as far as gender was concerned the M would be for "masculine" and the F for "feminine," and I didn't really see why it was any of their business. (The form provided no N, incidentally, which did reveal some of the confusion involved, since there actually is a third possible gender: "neuter"—very common in English; not present at all in French. Actually it might have been interesting to include it on the form, just to see what kind of responses it might elicit, to say nothing of what eyebrows those responses might in their turn send skyward!) But really that particular form was not interested in what role I occupied in society or the household—it wanted to know whether I was a man or a woman.

More recently, and far more absurdly, I was listening to a news report about the birth of a panda cub, and it was stated there that it would take several weeks before caretakers could discover what gender the cub would be. What **gender**?! Is that to say that in a few weeks it would be known what social, domestic, and professional roles the panda cub would one day be called upon to assume?! If it were to turn out to be a female, could she look forward to having to fret over being paid only 77% of what her equally qualified male counterparts were paid? Pandas have sexes, not genders—two, to be exact—each panda has only one; and that's that.

Even more recently yet, and perhaps more absurdly, I read of a (ho-hum, just another) Burmese python on the loose in swampy Florida, and in the article questions were raised about the python's *gender*. Now does anyone but the most dedicated herpetologist know, or care—or would even a herpetologist know what it *meant* to care about the social commitments and limitations of a male or female python (especially if it should happen to be at this moment tightening its grip around one's midsection)? Indeed we're all very grateful for that particular (real, honest-to-goodness) glass ceiling that keeps them in their place—both male and female—in the reptile zoo!

It has been said (and correctly so, I believe) that no matter how dissimilar two entities may appear to be, there are nevertheless certain traits, perhaps an indefinite number of them, that they share in common. So, what if I were to toss out, seemingly randomly, some mention of "academic journals" and place that alongside "Las Vegas"? Try as I might, the only common trait that comes to my mind between these two "things" is captured in the dictum "What happens there, stays there." In the case of Las Vegas, that phrase seems to be an affirmation that the city will honor your right to privacy. That is to say, no matter what a jackass you made of yourself while you were there, don't worry, no mention of it will ever make its way back to your home town (just by the way, I'm pretty sure this little slogan predates the advent and proliferation of social media). In the case of academic journals (sad to say, having been an academic myself), the phrase would simply indicate an overall societal indifference: who besides sociologists or philosophers themselves would ever dream of leafing through one of their journals? Nary such a publication is ever to be found sprawled on the table in a laundromat, among all the issues of *People*.

And yet somehow, exceptionally, this little terminological shift from "sex" to "gender" has managed to slip through the Guardians of Academe—perhaps in the furtive yet relentless manner in which the zebra mussel filtered into Lake Michigan—and it now wreaks similar havoc, if not ecologically, at least linguistically.

So at a time in our country's evolution when one can hardly turn on the television without confronting some mention or display or intimation of something pertaining to sex, the word itself seems to have been forced deep into the closet—to be applied, perhaps, only in reference to an *act*—hence the blushing (and when will that too become passé?)—but no more as the simple term of biological categorization that it always was. We may soon witness the emergence of a movement urging that we amend our Nineteenth Amendment so as to render it less salacious in guaranteeing that "the right of citizens of the United States to vote shall not be denied or abridged . . . on account of *gender*." Sex has no place in our sacred Constitution! The Founding Fathers would have been appalled!

Only of course they wouldn't have been. It was simply the idea of women voting that they would have rejected (had anyone in the room been bold enough to propose it in the first place).

Now is there anything *sexist* about anything I have said here? If so, I relish the thought, because it appears to be just a matter of time before that very word, which itself is not all that old, will be hounded out of our language, and replaced by the bloodless *genderist*. (But not yet, I am pleased to report, as a beautiful red line has just appeared under that last word, courtesy of my spellchecker.)

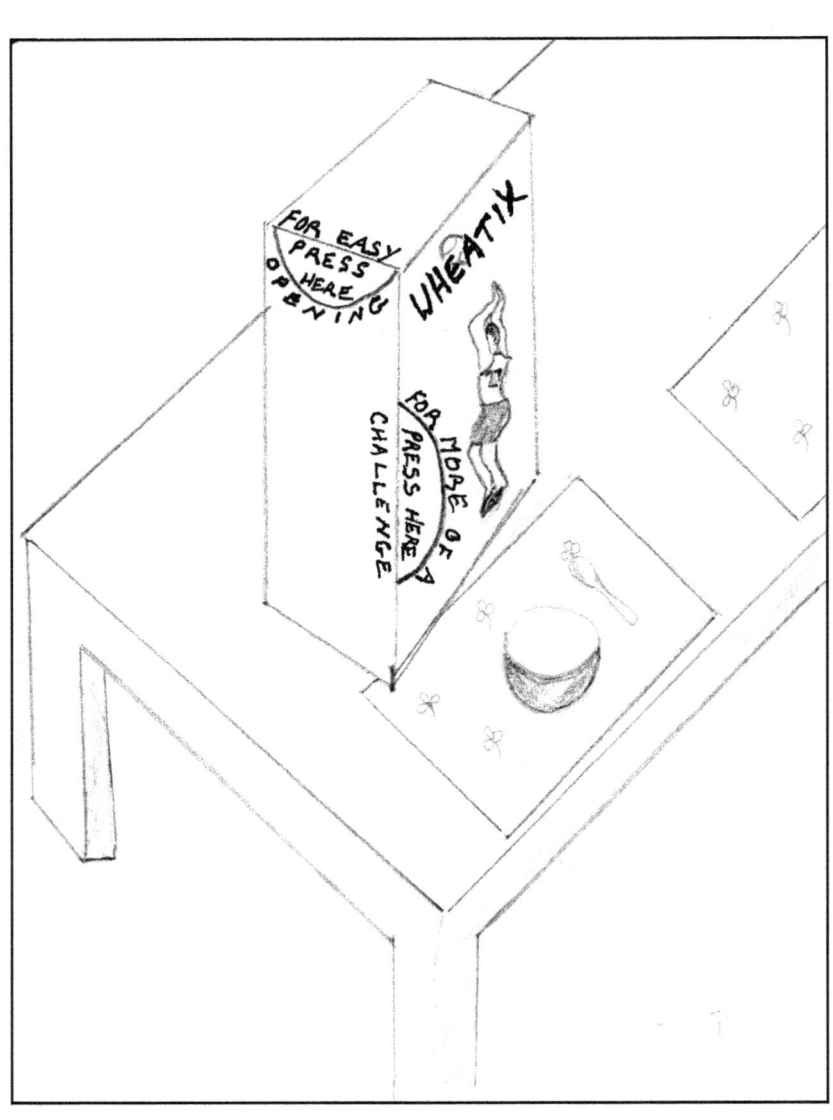

TROUBLE IN PARADISE

❧

The other day I descended our little mountain here in La Jolla down to the village below in my PT Cruiser, just to run a few errands. After a stop at the bank and the post office, I drove a couple blocks across town (a couple blocks across town, incidentally, = "to the other side of town") and parked in front of the drug store. A couple minutes later I came out of the drug store, got back in the car, and turned on the engine to head to my next destination. As the car started up I heard a light *thunk*, and on backing out I immediately discovered that I had no power steering.

Now the PT is small enough to control even without power steering, so I continued on with my chores undaunted (just the same, proceeding slowly and carefully!). When finished, I headed back up the mountain and reached home without incident. As this occurred late Friday afternoon, there was no getting the car to my mechanic until Monday, so I just parked it in the driveway, as I had been doing for several months at that time, and let it sit until Monday rolled around.

In the interim, I contemplated what might have gone wrong, but of course the extent of my contemplation in any such matter is limited by the extent of my automotive expertise, which in no way even merits the honorific accolade "sketchy." Given the suddenness of the incident, I figured there was no slow leak of fluid, but instead something must have snapped, or suddenly given way, doubtless in a hard-to-reach location (a redundancy when speaking of contemporary vehicles! Even if a part is right on top staring you in the face, odds are the critical screws—the ones that *just have to be turned*—are buried down below, and are probably accessible with a special tool that only the dealer possesses). Consequently, I reasoned, I should prepare myself for a rather stiff bill. So when Monday came I carefully navigated back down the hill (incidentally, given the mountainous topography involved, although my mechanic is 2 1/2 miles away, I could reach his shop even if I had no gas, or for that matter no gas *tank*), dropped the car off, and awaited the verdict.

Well, as it turned out, I was right in only one part of my informal diagnosis—something indeed had snapped. But it wasn't a belt, or a spring, or a support arm—in fact it wasn't any part of the engine, either moving or fixed; nor was it even any part of the car.

It was the neck of a rat.

The mechanic related that when he unbolted and lowered the pan to gain access to the engine from below, he found himself face to face with a dead rat, which I suppose is preferable to being face to face with a live rat, but not by a whole lot. What's more, he also attested to finding, on the upper side of the engine block, definite traces of a nest in the making. I suppose the location offered some warmth, and—what do I know?—maybe a bit of excitement, as well.

Apparently the rat had taken up residence under my hood (as I mentioned above, I had been keeping the car outside at this time), and on this fateful day had come along for a ride with me (perhaps he too had some errands in town—how long had this been going on?!). Apparently, also, he had picked just the wrong time to be nosing around in this new domicile of his, as he must have had his head up against the inside of the fan belt just at the moment I turned the ignition key. The belt, set into motion, strangled him immediately—that had to be the little *thunk* I heard. Still, in a way he had the last word, as in his ultimate gesture he succeeded in levering the fan belt from the spindle it rotates around, thereby disconnecting my power steering, and various other functions as well (cooling, for example) that are dependent on it.

So my mechanic needed only to reset the fan belt back onto its appropriate moorings, and I'd be good to go.

But of course he sold me a new fan belt. Oh well . . .

I leave it to the reader's creativity to discern a moral in all this. I can supply a touch of irony of my own, however, and it is this. I arrived late in life at the beautiful town of La Jolla—a town once described by Frank McShane (Raymond Chandler's biographer—Chandler resided here for many years) as "one of those American towns from which the ugly aspects of life have been carefully excluded." Ted Geisel (Dr. Seuss) lived here, too. The local playhouse was originally endowed by native son Gregory Peck. One of the principal cartographers responsible for mapping the human genome, L. Craig Venter, lives just down the street and around the corner. French/American sculptor Nikki de Saint-Phalle took up residence here, and has left many of her whimsical statues and constructions for our amusement in prominent and not-so-prominent places. (Come to think of it, I am *sooo* over my head here!)

Over the course of my life I have lived in small towns (Rockland, MA, Toms River, NJ), a big town (Lexington, KY), big cities (Boston, Paris).

And yet I never laid eyes on a single rat until I reached La Jolla.

PRIVATE ENEMY NUMBER ONE

The rat population, however, is really not the most annoying problem we confront in La Jolla—not in our house, at least. That distinction would seem to belong to the hummingbirds. No, I am not joking (though you can't prevent me from snickering a bit when I say this). At certain times of the year—perhaps clustering around the migration-to-Mexico and the migration-out-of-Mexico periods—we can expect to be called upon to evict on average one hummingbird a week from our living room, or even the kitchen (where it's never an easy task, as the only windows the birds can fly toward are 16 feet above the floor). Being the most nimble fliers in all of bird-dom, you can imagine that this poses a major challenge. And a hummingbird is not something you can ignore—like a simple house fly that can be allowed to bang away insensibly at a pane of glass as long as it pleases. The hummingbird commands attention and requires action. But more on this shortly.

For the benefit of anyone reading this who comes from the east, or the south, or for that matter the north, or the west, an explanation is in order as to how a hummingbird can get into the house in the first place. "Even if the windows are left open," you might be wondering, "how do they get through the screens?" And the short answer to that query is "What screens?"

Now in all the other places I have lived (New Jersey, Massachusetts, and a long stretch in Kentucky), the windows could be kept open for only a few days out of the year: too cold in winter—must keep the house closed up tight (to seal the heat in)—too hot in summer—must keep the house closed up tight (to avoid straining the A/C). In none of those locations was there ever all that much spring to speak of, as up north the winters tended to shoulder spring out of the way until about mid-May, when it would allow a couple days of it to seep through before handing the (hot, soggy) ball off to summer, while in the south summer would assert its dominion fairly early on, overpowering all but the first few days of springtime. So maybe there were a couple days you could open the windows to clear the stale winter air out of the house—but of course you had to take care not to leave them open if you were planning to be away for a few hours, as there's no telling when a storm might rumble through.

Autumn did provide a slightly longer stretch of tolerable, dry weather, so let's say out of 365 days maybe 15 invited or at least permitted one to open up the house to the fresh air. But even then the screens had to be kept in place, as both spring and fall are prime mosquito seasons, and one marauding mosquito can easily ruin a whole night's sleep.

By contrast, we have no screens in our windows here, and we often keep them wide open for several hours in the day, with no restrictions on what months that can occur in. For example it is January 21 when I am writing this, and both sliding doors plus the door to the patio stand fully open, and there is nothing exceptional in that.

The reason screens are irrelevant here is that there are very few flying insects around, and no mosquitoes. Temperature control inside the house can be accomplished through manipulation of the openness of the windows at different times of the day, at different times of the year. Just to illustrate this dearth of flying insects, there is a large street light in a parking lot about 50' from our living room—an ideal location, you might think, for a spider to spin a web and catch her fill of moths and other winged delights. I remember when one did just that, a very large spider (though perhaps the glare of the light made her look larger yet). I watched as she wove her beautiful trap ever so skillfully—artfully—then stepped aside to wait for the clientele to start showing up, rather like a *maître d'* standing entreatingly (yet ever so professionally) alongside the door of his restaurant on opening night, shoulders squared, towel folded neatly over his arm. She maintained vigil for a couple weeks (so did I, but not so intently, I can guarantee), then either starved to death or simply relocated, as not once did I ever witness the ensnaring of a passing insect, or even see any circling around the light out of harm's way; and because of its brightness they would be easy to spot. So in short, there is little to prevent us from keeping our doors and windows open wide during much of the day time.

Now there are usually a few flower arrangements in the living room, and it must be they which draw the hummingbirds across the threshold and into the house for a closer inspection. Color and shape appear to attract them, for there is another arrangement, this one of artificial flowers, that stands just outside the dining room door on the patio, and innumerable times I have sat and watched as a hummingbird comes to those "flowers," pokes its beak into one then another of them, then with a "What wuz I thinkin'?!" shudder, darts off in search of something genuinely organic.

Amazing factoid: According to Sibley's (Audubon Society approved) Guide to Birds, *the average weight of an Anna's hummingbird (our local variety) is 0.15 oz.*

Disturbing corollary no. 1: If you could somehow fit six(!) such birds into a normal-sized envelope (shudder!) you could mail them to any of the 50 states using only one first class stamp. In fact you could probably even include a note without getting into the second ounce—a note that perhaps explained what led you to do such a thing in the first place.

Disturbing corollary no. 2: The brain of the average hummingbird would seem to weigh roughly as much as your weekly pile of fingernail clippings.

And therein lies the problem. Magnificent little flying machines that our mighty Air Force can only *dream* of emulating, when they are in their proper element, hovering from flower to (real) flower, and extracting whatever it is that they extract with their needle-like beaks, they are models of efficiency—Intelligent Design, the theists would tell us. But through all that they are under the sage guidance of instinct, which thousands and thousands of years of trial and error, failure and success, has ultimately managed to inscribe in their very DNA. Just let some novel phenomenon intrude into their world, however, one that nowhere appears on the checklist of instinctual responses—say, a simple pane of glass—and all the fine tuning wrought by Natural Selection is at once annulled, leaving the poor creature to rely on its intelligence, its *brain*—remember that pile of fingernails alluded to?

"Madam/Sir: You just came through a door that stands six feet high and four feet wide; now as you hover only a few feet away from this gaping aperture you conclude that you have had your fill of the nourishment you entered in search of. Won't you please just shift into reverse gear—a maneuver only you in the entire avian kingdom, you this 1/6 oz. marvel, can perform!—and quickly but gracefully ease out of the area the way you came in?" Alas, all its ancestral lessons are at once forgotten, and banging its beak against the nearest pane of glass while humming its wings in exhausting, ever-shortening spurts becomes the preferred answer to this newly encountered, unexpected predicament.

And if there is one instinctual element in their behavior that is often triggered by such a circumstance, and which does bear the imprimateur of intelligent design, it is this: Remove yourself as far as possible from that most dreadful of enemies, the Human Being. Yet it turns out that in this case—an irony lost on this mini-marvel—the only hope our poor creature has of surviving the ordeal it has inflicted on itself and cannot think its own way out of, is precisely one of these dreaded predators—*me!*

I have developed quite effective catch and release techniques over the years. This year for some reason they seem to head toward a window which, while fixed, at least stands close to an openable one, and one which is feet-on-the-ground accessible. I need but coax them with a feather duster over to this other window that I have just opened wide, until their stupidity surrenders the upper hand, and they can dart back into their familiar world. This technique overrides the paper bag method that is called for when no such egress is proximate. However, when they head for those windows near the apex of our A-frame ceiling, about 16 feet above the floor, then their life, and to a real but lesser extent the life of their savior, is put at risk. Up there they will just buzz against the window until absolute exhaustion overtakes them, and they expire "for good" (a neighbor told me that painters had once discovered a tiny feathered carcass on the shelf below the high-up windows in their living room).

The time the hummingbird selected the kitchen windows to be his final resting place, I was at least able to climb up on the counter and stabilize myself against the cabinets. That brought me within maybe seven feet of the window ledge, so using the soft mop with the extension shaft that I employ when scrubbing out-of-the-way corners of the house, or removing cobwebs from same, I figured I could harass him into relocating to a more accessible place. And so I did. It took a lot of harassing, but finally the little fellow abandoned his post and half fell half fluttered down to the top of the cabinet, where he lay motionless, wings akimbo, all fight and flight drained out of his tiny body. We were eye to eye, his little beak quivering, and he seemed to be saying "Enough! Just end it now. *Please!*"

So I carefully positioned my paper bag, gave him a gentle snap with one finger—one must be ever mindful of how eminently crushable a 1/6 oz. creatures is—and quickly sealed up the bag once he was in it. Then I could climb down from the counter, take my captive outside, and set him loose back into the world that made sense to him. I don't know which of us was more exhausted, thankful and relieved at the conclusion of this ordeal, but I do know that immediately upon release, this particular hummingbird flew away faster, further, *straighter* than I have ever seen one of them fly.

But the Mother of All Rescues was effected in the living room, again up at the 16-foot windows, but where there is no counter to climb up on, so any harassment had to be performed up on a ladder. And I do not enjoy time spent on ladders. There was, in addition, a brilliant bit of "engineering" involved—in effect turning a window into a blank wall—all credit for which goes to my wife who hatched the idea.

For this operation I had been obliged to bring the taller of my ladders up from the garage, and to rearrange the furniture in order to accommodate it, just to put myself in a position to employ the same technique I had used in the kitchen, involving the soft mop with the extension shaft. So I flailed away at where I figured the bird was. I couldn't really see—I think this one was a "her"—due to the width of the window ledge she would rest on, but every time I succeeded in provoking her into action she would just flutter to the other side of the ledge and bang away at the glass futilely (both windows in the living room are six feet wide, so with each successive flutter I would have to reposition my ladder and myself to begin again).

Sensing that futility aptly described both the bird's efforts and my own, it suddenly occurred to my wife, who was witnessing this spectacle, that if only we could cover over the windows—both of the six-foot windows in the room—thereby rendering them opaque, the bird's (imagined) connection with the outside world would be severed. She would have no further incentive to bang against the glass till death "did her part," and might seek to relocate to a different window—one equally futile, of course, but at least accessible to me.

I remembered that we had a roll of black plastic left behind by some workmen a couple years earlier that they had used to keep from tramping dirt across a rug they were working near. All I had to do (Heh! *"All I had to do . . . !"*)

was cart the ladder I had been using back down the stairs and outside to the base of the garage roof. There I could tuck the roll of black plastic under one arm, then climb up to the apex of the roof—about a 30 foot climb, but at least not a steep one. Then I unrolled about 15 feet of plastic, cut it off, and affixed it to the upper ridge of the roof using that ultimate handyman's panacea, duct tape. And bingo!—a wall had been created, and hopefully the window would thereby lose its allure.

I then climbed back down, dismounted the roof, hauled the ladder back up to the living room, and recommenced harassment, hoping this time for more positive results. Such results were not long in coming. The bird rather quickly soured on her current location, saw the light (so to speak—light provided by the darkness that suddenly engulfed her—there are ironies all over the place in this tale, aren't there?!), and fluttered down, coming to rest on another ledge, this one about five feet above the floor. Once again I found myself eye to eye with a motionless hummingbird, utterly exhausted and bereft of hope; once again I saw that supplicating look in her eyes as she lay there motionless—that "You win. *No más!*" look. And once again I was able to snap her into a waiting bag and ferry her across the room to freedom. This time it was with relief that I again mounted the roof, climbed to the top and removed the black plastic, descended, and went back inside—where I could take the ladder to its nook in the garage, return the furniture once again to its proper position, and collapse onto the sofa in an exhausted heap.

The Beat Goes On. By an interesting coincidence—only a coincidence this time, no irony involved—just as I was writing this (somewhere in the midst of about a four hour interlude that occurred between the paragraph on page 68 that ended with the sentence "For example it is January 21 . . ." and the one that begins "The reason screens are irrelevant . . .") I was brought to attention by that familiar FRRRRRRRRRRR sound, and knew right away I would have to—you guessed it!—evict another hummingbird. A beautiful male Anna's hummingbird, wearing that characteristic iridescent hot pink scarf around his neck, at least the defenestration proved to be a simple operation this time—no ladders involved, no surrender on his part: just a simple feather duster, an open window, and a flight to freedom.

Now how long will it be before my next *mano a ala* confrontation?!

BEAR WITH ME (TO THE END)

Having been led on a business trip to the city of Vancouver a few years back, and finding ourselves with a couple days to ourselves before taking the return flight home, my wife and I decided to rent a car and explore the region a bit—in particular, to see what Vancouver Island had to offer. We presumed it would be very beautiful, and we were not mistaken in that presumption. The month was May, which for such a place had the added attraction of being between seasons; consequently, the winter crowd, with all traces of ice and snow having vanished, was no longer to be seen, while the invaders of summer, soon to make their landing on the beachhead, were yet to arrive.

Indeed, we practically did have the island to ourselves. We dined at a restaurant where only one other table was occupied, after which we lazily headed back to our (practically empty) motel. Along the way, though, we noticed a sign that pointed out the direction to the shore, and with the sun close to setting we thought there might be some spectacular views to take in, and maybe a few memorable pictures to snap. Again, we presumed correctly.

We pulled into a parking lot which was tastefully buried in the underbrush. Clearly that was arranged with the intent of shielding any beachgoers from the sight of a sea of automobiles that might compromise their experience of Brute Nature. (Oh, Canada! . . .) But on this particular evening the sea of automobiles consisted precisely of one—ours. Finding our way to a narrow pathway that had been cut through the brush, and which led to the beach, we followed it a short distance until a long sandy stretch bordering the Pacific suddenly came into view--one that to all appearances belonged entirely to us. It formed a gentle arc that extended, I would judge, about five or six miles, some to the north of where we entered, some to the south, bracketed at each extremity by a jutting cluster of rocks and trees.

The sun was closing in on the horizon, so we set out walking in the sand at a leisurely pace, waiting for the sun to stop merely descending and begin disappearing. That would make for the most striking photos, I figured. The peaceful evening, the mild atmosphere, the deserted beach and gentle surf all conduced to our falling into a reverie of sorts that left us unsure after a while whether we had been walking five or 15, or 20 minutes—and we did reverse direction at one point, but was it early on, halfway through . . . ? In any case, the sun finally lost itself beneath the horizon, I had taken enough pictures, so we decided it was time to call it a blissful evening and head back to the car. Such at least was our intent.

However, as we reached the thicket of brush where we thought we would find the path leading back to the parking lot, we found only . . . thicket. Looking along it to the left and right as far as our gaze could reach, no breach in the wall of greenery could be detected, and I used the phrase "*wall* of greenery," with care and intent, for wherever you stood you could not see more than a couple feet into it, and couldn't possibly, without the aid of a machete, ever think of passing through it.

It was at that moment that a question and a fact simultaneously presented themselves to my consciousness, causing my emotions to shift into a gear they were massively unwilling to accept. The question: Just how far *had* we walked from wherever it was that we entered onto the sand, and had we entered to the north or the south of where we now found ourselves? (Well, I guess that's two questions; or three. But however many questions were involved, they all pointed to a state of bewilderment.) The fact: The sun was now below the horizon, hence, but a few minutes of daylight remained to us. And as impenetrable as the wall of brush was in broad daylight, it would be ever so much more so in the dark.

Lethargic from the heavy meal we had just consumed, I suddenly realized that if I couldn't find the pathway to the parking lot *right now*, we would be spending the night alone on the beach, utterly unprepared for any such "outing." This realization shot through me as if I had just latched barehanded onto a live wire, and immediately shook me from lethargy into sprint mode. And yet I wasn't even sure in which direction I should be sprinting! Where had we stepped onto the sand, on this several-miles-long, largely undifferentiated stretch of beach? If I set out running in the wrong direction, I would waste not only the time spent in futile pursuit, but an equal amount of time in returning to where I had started out. And the approaching darkness was not going to retard its advance just to accommodate me! Oh, I know, the Lord did hold the sun in place for several hours one day--long enough for Joshua and his band of merry men to slaughter their fill of Amorites--but somehow I didn't think He was prepared or disposed to extend the same courtesy to me.

Since the major portion of the strand extended to the

north, I started running in that direction, at a pace way faster than my stomach was comfortable with. I kept it up for a few minutes, but as you might expect, nothing positive turned up. And of course I had left my wife planted in the sand back where I had started, as she could hardly have kept up with the frantic pace I had set for myself. I cannot remember ever having felt so utterly desperate—and to think how closely that feeling followed on the heels of the satiated contentment I had been afloat in barely moments ago!

I abandoned my northward trajectory, and on turning around to head back toward the south again, retracing my strides, I made a wonderful discovery: we were not alone on the beach! Far down, almost to the lower rocky terminus of the sandy stretch, I spotted another couple perhaps half a mile away ambling unconcernedly along the water's edge. Their seeming insouciance informed me that they *had* to know where the egress was—either that or they hadn't yet realized what peril they were in. I chose to believe the former, and lit out toward them, faster yet, as I had to be sure of reaching them while there was still a bit of the evening light left—I would *not* let them out of my sight! It took a few minutes for me to even begin to draw close to them, and I wondered if they were wondering what this person heading frantically toward them had on his mind—whether I came as friend or foe. I knew I would arrive red-faced and panting, and I just was hoping they weren't armed and alarmed. (Though what could I have been thinking—this was Canada, not Texas, eh!)

When I at last reached them I breathlessly explained my plight and asked if they knew where the parking lot was. They indicated its whereabouts with a nod, as it turned out to be much closer to the southern extremity of the beach than I had imagined (hence my mad dash northwards was only self-defeating). I headed off in the direction they indicated, in the ever-waning light, and did find a pathway that led to a parking lot . . . but there was no car there. No matter this time, though—I could see that several parking areas were strung together like beads, and so following the thread for a minute or so I did at last arrive at the lot where our car stood, in splendid isolation.

Now I had only to dash back to fetch my wife and guide her across the sand to the little hidden path that had proved so elusive, before the night swallowed it, and us, up completely. My ordeal was over.

But as if to add an exclamation point to the entire experience, as I made my way down the path to the beach one last time, I happened to look up and glimpse a sign that had escaped my notice earlier. It read:

CAUTION
STAY OFF BEACH AT NIGHT
BEARS IN THE AREA

It was not until we had been back home in Lexington for a few weeks that I as much as dared to open my mouth about this little detail.

NOTES ON THE IMPOSSIBLE

This and the following two pieces cling loosely to one another not in any essential way, but through the contingent fact that they all derive from my years spent in France. Those were eye-opening times for me, during which I learned how to look at and look for things of beauty and visual interest—faculties that had lain largely dormant in my life here in the U.S. But as you will see, the lessons I came away with, and experiences I underwent reached far beyond the (merely) aesthetic realm.

After an initial immersion into France and "the French way"—which often had the feel of a baptism by fire—I found my way to loving the country perhaps more than a great many of its natural residents, and was ecstatic when we actually bought a small apartment in Paris *and became taxpayers there*! It must to be love, you have to think, if you *enjoy* paying taxes. Perhaps this state of mind grew in no small measure from the fact that I never had to work there, never had to show up at a job. Thanks to the excellent public transportation the people enjoy there, I was never even obliged to drive a car through the streets of the city, which to all appearances could often be a hair-tearing task. I was, you might say, "out on my own recognizance." And perhaps, in a curious way, I was able to enjoy the beauties of the city and the countryside because the people there always treated me like a foreigner. Everywhere I have lived here, from coast to coast in this big country of ours, I have *felt* like a foreigner, hence have always been out of step with a populace that saw me as one of their own ("So what's wrong with *him*?"). But this was the first and only instance where I genuinely *merited treatment* as a foreigner. *At last I had found a home!*

Darkness in the City of Lights

The voyage to this state of mind, however, was at times a stormy one. Just for example, if you ever spend any substantial amount of time in France, one of the commonest words you will hear in any form of transaction, and one of the easiest to remember, because it usually comes first, is "no." (Well actually it is *"non,"* but that second "n" lives only on paper, and falls by the wayside when uttered—a fate that befalls many letters or strings of letters in spoken French, like the "ent" in *"parlent"* or *"restaient."*) Right alongside *"non"* in frequency, and often following immediately upon it in discourse, is the word *"impossible."* Thus whatever request you may have made is likely to be greeted by the reply "Non . . . im-pos-sible!" each syllable being carved with precision—highlighted, as it were—so they can be savored (by the speaker) and absorbed (by the listener), both individually and as part of the declaration as a whole.

Given that many a transaction begins in this fashion, it is reasonable to expect that many transactions never really . . . transact. When a door is slammed in your face, you have to *really want* whatever stands on the other side of the door, to summon forth the courage to knock again. And some days it just might not seem worth the trouble. This is unfortunate. For there is a proverb that over time you will also hear repeated again and again there, and it says

"Il n'y a rien d'impossible en France"—"There is nothing in France that is impossible."

On my first extended visit to France it was the negative, the *impossible*, that overpowered me. It seemed as if at each turn I would run headlong into "No; can't be done"; "Not open today"; "Don't know where it is"; "Can't be done"; "Can't be done"; **"Can't be done!"**

Naturally I took all this negativity literally and personally. It had to be because I was an American, I reasoned. After all, they knew nothing of me as a person, but apparently it was difficult to conceal my Americanness, and they just didn't care to be accommodating to Americans. I figured they had all heard, only too often, "You owe us!" . . . "You owe us!", and had grown tired of being reminded of their boundless indebtedness. So was I buffeted about on my first go at life in France; forced, I surmised, to suffer for the sins of my compatriots—sins indeed which were numerous and visible.

"An American just takes up much more space than any of us does," I was to hear, and with space coming at such a premium throughout all Europe, it was clearly not intended as a complimentary remark. But had I not seen that to be the case on my very first flight over, when I sat across the aisle from an American family with two small children? By the time we landed they had filled their seating area and the aisle with such a selection of toys and games that it seemed they must all have been drawn from some magical sack, much like that bottomless flask which Odysseus used in plying the Cyclops with so much wine that the monster would be "anesthetized" when the moment came to perform a little emergency ocular surgery on him. Shortly after this experience I found myself in a railway compartment, seated face to face with a family of similar size and configuration, only French. "Not again!" I lamented silently. "Why me?!" But as it turned out, my lamentations were unnecessary, for the French children spoke softly, ate neatly, and played reservedly.

Many years later, a Frenchman (who was just about to rent our house in the U.S. while we were leaving for another sabbatical in his home country) explained to me, "We treat children as we treat trees: in France we plant them [the trees, that is] neatly in rows and shape them carefully as they grow; in America they are allowed to grow and spread however their nature dictates." I confess I never did care much for French arboreal topiary, but I could only laud its application in the domain of child rearing.

And we take up auditory space, as well. I have been in a restaurant in Paris where a single table of Americans filled the room in a manner that rendered anyone else's *sotto voce* interchanges impossible—it was shout now or simply hold your peace. Such a blessed hush fell over the room when that table finally emptied out, and the sound of silence once again allowed polite conversation to resume!

So I steeled myself to withstand the wave of negativity that seemed everywhere to threaten to engulf me. I couldn't wait to return to my own country where clerks and vendors would smile their vapid smiles and wish me a nice day as if they really cared. (Recently I have observed a change in tactics here, and instead of being wished a nice day, I am asked to comment on how my day has been going. So now the burden of supplying saccharine commentary falls on me, and not the clerk or teller or whoever—unless I opt for the truth, to wit: (a) I haven't really noticed; (b) better than yours, or (c) that's hardly your business.) Yes, this was the world I longed to return to, from which you can easily infer the extent to which I was socially shell-shocked.

In the face of this apparent onslaught of negativity some question must arise as to how and why I should become attached to such a place, become a property owner, spend years of my life there. And I can only say that enlightenment did come to me, though not in an instant. It required seeing beyond the moment, reflecting on events, expanding my view to reach beyond myself and the little everyday confrontations I underwent—in short, I slowly developed a feel for this new environment.

The Path to Enlightenment

Step 1 – I Am Not Alone

I came to see that my Americanness had nothing to do with the overdose of attitude I had been reacting to. The French are just a quarrelsome people, and in fact they showed themselves again and again to be equal opportunity quarrelers. Like one of the old Green Bay Packers once famously said of Coach Lombardi, "He treated us all equally . . . like dogs!" Standing in line at the post office proved to be a prime spot to watch for explosions, as back in my first days and, for that matter, years it was remarkably poorly organized—a pile of dried leaves just awaiting that stray spark to touch it off. I observed numerous heated exchanges between clerks and clients, none of which involved me, nor other Americans, or even other foreigners. Just the same, I took to making my visits to the post office very early in the day, before lines would grow long and tempers short.

Supermarket lines were also volatile spots. I observed

one interchange between an elderly lady and the girl at the register that terminated with the girl calling the lady a *cochon* (pig!). (Were such a scene as that to unfold over here, that one word would likely have been the last word the clerk was to say while still in the employ of the market. Over there, well, let's not overreact, OK?) The interpersonal atmosphere I was immersed in over there crackled in a far more lively way than the one I had been brought up in here, and even (lowly) clerks were allowed to have feelings, and to let them bubble over into public view on occasion. They simply would not become have-a-nice-day automatons. The mantra so often chanted over here is "It's a free country, right?" but how many low- to mid-level employees can safely allow the slightest shard of their personal or emotional lives to make any appearance in the workplace? Over there I once overheard one saleslady voicing to another a little ditty they had been taught, so they might always be on their good behavior: *"Le client est là, et le client est roi"* (The client is before you, and he is king")—a rhyming version of our "The customer is always right." Then both of them fell to tittering, as if to say "What silliness!" Ultimately I came to enjoy the little flareups I witnessed as evidence of *life* manifested in individual freedoms, and when that life happened to boil up and singe me a bit, I came to accept it with equanimity.

Step 2 – Two Girls and a Chicken
Let us take careful note here: How often does a chicken occupy a pivotal position on any "path to enlightenment"? I'm just wondering.

It's funny how one small incident can shed so much light on so much more—like if you were to crack open a door an inch or so and, on peeking in, discover that a massive surprise party was being planned on your behalf. One day, during the phase when my exasperation level was very high, I had ordered a roasted chicken from a nearby *boucherie*. (Somehow that sounds much more alluring than "butcher shop." At that epoch, incidentally, this particular *boucherie* stood right next door to a *chevaline*: a *boucherie* that dealt exclusively in horse meat! This was in 1980. Such shops were soon to vanish.) When I arrived at the shop to pick it up (while the rest of dinner sat on the table back in the apartment), my request seemed to bewilder the young woman sitting at the register. "Chicken? Let's see; Manns, you say?" And as she scanned down some list she had in front of her she announced "I don't see anything like that here. *Désolée!*" "*Désolée*," I had come to learn, was the word they used as an ellipsis for "I can't tell you how happy I am to report that I can be of no service to you!"

Apparently my displeasure started to make itself visible—something quite unusual for me—as another employee who had been off at a certain distance, but who clearly had been listening to the exchange, chimed in *"Ah, oui,* that's right—that's it over there, and she indicated the whereabouts of the bird with her chin, thinking she was imparting information to her colleague. But a blush, a furtive look and the hint of a snicker told me at once that she knew about it all along, and had just been playing cat and mouse with me. What an absolute doofus I had been. I was being teased, but nothing more. My getting upset was the desired result.

How long had this been going on? I couldn't then remember all the instances where meaningless roadblocks had been thrown in my way, so I *certainly* can't now. And it wasn't easy to retrospectively revoke all the excrudescences of ill-will that such teasings had occasioned in me. But at least I was confident that the next time something of the sort arose, it was an invitation to play along—and as good a way as any to improve one's French!

So Lesson One taught me that most of the time I was not being singled out for hostility or derision; I was more like a random fly alighting on an electrified grid. And now Lesson Two taught me that even when I *was* being singled out, it was only for the sake of toying with me, and toying back was fair play. I could only wish it had all been that harmless, once upon a time, on the grade school playgrounds in Toms River!

Step Three – At the Foot of the Master

Eventually I had adjusted enough to these new modes of behavior to conceive the dream of acquiring a small hideaway in Paris for us to retreat to every so often (a *pied-à-terre* they call it—"foot on the ground"), and that dream actually became a reality a couple years later. We bought a small apartment in the west end of the city (near the *Bois de Boulogne*), and set about to put our own stamp on it. It was small enough that this wasn't an insuperable challenge; nor, however, was it a mere walk in the park (or in this case the *Bois*). The building had been constructed in the 1930s, and was heated by hot water coursing through radiators— one per room, which in our case totaled one. This one radiator was parked under a picture window, which prevented the use of floor-length curtains, and a window of that size wearing in effect a miniskirt was somehow less than elegant. And did we not seek, in Paris, a touch of elegance? Naturally it was my wife who had the eyes to see what was needed, and the will to see it through to realization. This proved to be a major confrontation with *l'impossible*, but one that simply had to be overcome. And yet in the end it provided us with a clear look, up close and personal, of why it just might be true that nothing is impossible in France.

To displace a radiator in a big building of which you only own a tiny part is no small challenge. First we had to receive permission to do such a thing from the homeowners' association; then we had to line up people to execute it, and that was a larger problem yet. Someone like a building superintendent had to come and shut off the water to the overall heating system, perhaps even to the building as a whole, and remain around to turn it back on, once the plumber—who had agreed to come at the same time as the superintendent in order to loosen, relocate, and retighten the apparatus—had completed his phase of the operation. Fortunately this was all to occur in August, when at least no heating was actually taking place.

Unfortunately this was all to occur in *August,* for August in Paris is notorious for being a month of little accomplishment—most of its residents are on vacation and somewhere else; the city more or less belongs to the tourists, and a neighborhood such as ours which was well off the path beaten by tourists had the look of a ghost town. And yet our mission (which we chose to accept) required that we (1) prevail upon the lady who was heading up the homeowners' association (thankfully she hadn't yet left for *her* vacation!), (2) to prevail upon the building superintendent not only to come shut off the water, but to (3) prevail upon the plumber of his choice to come and meet him at the site in order to perform the above-mentioned series of tasks—as quickly as possible, of course, to give least inconvenience to whatever other residents might be present, i.e., not on vacation themselves. (4) In Paris. (5) In August.

It was our great fortune that the lady who occupied the axial position in this operation was willing to hear us out and immediately became sympathetic to our request. Had she herself been cantankerous, it might never have come off. So maybe to one-up the impossible, you sometimes need a little luck. Actually, though, I had been coming to feel that, contrary to my initial sentiments and to an opinion widely held, we Americans are not the hated species we are often made out (usually by ourselves) to be, but even enjoy certain advantages. This is especially the case if you are willing to have a go at their beloved language, and are disinclined toward any chest-thumping arrogance, the sort of behavior that, for example, I witnessed once in a bank, where a man (an American, of course) was practically shouting to one of the tellers **"What's the matter? Don't you speak English?"** *(!?!)* But the French did seem to have an almost secret respect—even admiration—for us: perhaps it's our can-do attitude (the very attitude we were hoping to coax from the lady before us at that very moment); perhaps a certain freedom from restraint in our actions (a French person once told me how they were always fearful of the *"ce qu'on dit"*—the talk that goes on, or *might* go on about them behind their backs, and that forever constricts their behavior). Or could it not be that they just might secretly harbor a wish to "take up as much space as an American"? Whatever the explanation, a little French and a peaceful smile can carry you a long way. (And when, many years after the scene I'm depicting unfolded, tragedy struck in our land—to be precise, on 9–11–01— their country wept soulful tears on our behalf. And with what remarkably quickness was our government able to turn such mellow wine to vinegar!)

End of digression. The lady proceeded to give us an admirable demonstration of how to go about inducing the inflexible to bend. Indeed she truly went to war for us, engulfing her interlocutor with wave after wave of unctuous entreaties. Each new assault began with an "Ah, Jean . . . *écouuuute* . . . " ("*listen*," something which Jean appeared ill-disposed to doing, given how frequently she had to resort to that phrase); "they're just the nicest people . . . !" And we were, of course, but she had not really had enough exposure to us to know that. The wheedling and importuning went on and on—this Jean seemed to be one tough nut to crack! But crack he did at last; our spokeswoman apparently had melted his icy resolve, and the operation was to take place soon (in fact Jean or his confederate or both appeared on the verge of heading out for their own vacation). It came off without a hitch, though not without a little obligatory grumping on the part of both the super and the plumber.

I knew I could never be as obsequious as the lady had been—in fact I'm quite sure that for a man to do so would be repulsive and counterproductive—but I did learn that it is at times expedient if not necessary to set your own pride aside, only temporarily, in order to gratify the pride of someone else. And who doesn't need a little puffing up once in a while? In the end you get what you want and they get what they want. Actually, though, I got the feeling that both sides in the interchange I witnessed understood it was a game they were playing, and that in some mysterious way the game was bigger than either of them, yet they were powerless to resist engaging in it. I have no doubt that when all was said and done, both felt a bit better for their participation.

So at last I saw the phrase *"Non! . . . Impossible!"* not as a harsh rejection, but simply as the opening gambit in an exchange that may take an occasional unexpected turn, but which, with proper navigational skills, would lead to a resolution, and not just one that involved a cold concession, on someone's part—a surrender—but rather a genuine accommodation. Barriers that on first sight appeared to be impervious ultimately were not broken down, but melted away.

Step Four - With a Little Help from My Friends

Time, of course, passed; and with its passage came an ever-increasing sense of being at home in this once foreign, "hostile" environment. I can recall no unhappy confrontations after we had "settled in." Whether I was responsible for this—my own adjustments—or the French themselves were mellowing, would be hard to quantify. I did read on occasion of the efforts made in France to soften their *"acceuil"*—"welcome"—since their GNP is heavily dependent on tourism. The dreaded post office, for example, was streamlined to avoid bottlenecks and the outbreaks they would give rise to. Disney World opened up a short train ride outside Paris, and the young employees who welcomed visitors and guided them around were actually being taught how to greet people with a smile, not a sneer (sadly, "mellowing" did at times take on the appearance of falling into the "have a nice day" syndrome).

On the other hand, it might simply have been the case that I had developed a certain finesse in steering around the various speed bumps that can appear in one's path.

(The French, incidentally, have a cute term for what we call speed bumps: *"gendarmes couchés"*—sleeping policemen!) When one is emboldened by the conviction that nothing is impossible, suddenly (surprisingly) nothing *is* impossible: *Zen and the Art of Intercultural Relations.*

Now I was at a certain time engaged in a bit of research into a cluster of nineteenth-century French philosophers who had adopted and were carrying on a philosophical approach that had come to flourish in the century previous to that in Scotland. This "certain time" actually extended over a few years, and led me to become a denizen of such grand establishments as the *Bibliothêque Nationale*, and the library at the Sorbonne. Both of these required my acquiring a library card, but that involved only wading through some rather shallow and tepid bureaucracy. Once approved, I had access to a massive sea of writings, a great many of which had not been touched for—who knows?—maybe a century or more (or ever—one that I recall having delivered to my desk was a copy autographed by the author himself and dedicated to the Dean of the University; and the pages in it had not yet been slashed!). Indeed often my first order of business, when a book was brought to me, was to blow away the column of dust that had accumulated along its upper edge. (And if it was clean at the outset, that was immediate cause for suspicion—who might be trying to get a jump on my research project?!) I still retain this attraction toward dusty books. I can breeze through a store filled with new publications in a matter of seconds, but will linger at much greater length in one that invites the wearing of gloves and a dust mask.

Even the card catalog at the Sorbonne was a delight, although no doubt the digital era has done away with the hard copy that filled countless drawers. But back then, not only were all the cards hand-written, but many of them, especially those recording the type of book I was seeking out, were written in *italics*! Hand-written italicized cards pointing the way to dust-encrusted books—it doesn't get any better than that!

I had even behaved ingratiatingly enough, apparently, to earn a tour of the special collections section, and it was there that I happened to make a discovery that would lead me to put the "nothing is impossible" adage to a serious test. I had been researching the influence of an eighteenth century Scottish school of philosophy known as Commonsense, upon nineteenth century French thinkers; but I came by chance across a reference to a seventeenth-century French philosopher who also was said to be an advocate of common sense (a much more rigorous term in philosophy, incidentally, than in everyday discourse). "Wouldn't it be marvelous," I mused, "if in truth the Scot I had been treating as the point of origin had himself been shaped by some French predecessor?" What a delightfully unexpected circle that would make! I had to know his works—to possess a copy of them, in fact, and not just struggle through them in the library.

The catch here however was that, having no formal connection with the Sorbonne, pursuing this project entirely on my own, I was not permitted to leave the library with any of its holdings. And with but one heavily used copy machine at the disposal of everyone there, making a copy myself was out of the question. As it happened, by no coincidence whatever, a copy shop was situated right across the street from the library. If only I could place the book in their hands for a few hours! "Nothing is impossible" I reminded myself.

Now there was a position in the library known as the *chef de la salle* (that "*chef*" just means "chief," by the way, not "cook"), occupied in this instance by a woman whose desk was literally "on high"—the most prominent location in the entire room, from which, in one sweeping glance, she could take in any and all proceedings in the area below. If I could induce her to give her blessing to my leaving the premises with the volume in question for only a couple hours I would be home free. God knows how long it had been since anyone had so much as glanced at it! I knew very well, though, what her initial response would be.

"Impossible!" Pawn to K4. No problem; she must be seen to put up stiff resistance, after all—nothing less could be expected from the *chef de la salle*. I explained my situation in a manner that I thought would elicit most sympathy.

"Impossible!" I offered to leave something of mine behind (I forget what) as collateral. (That maneuver had worked for me once back in the 60s, when I was a young idiot driving from Boston to New Jersey on Christmas Eve with no money in my pocket, no credit cards, and no gas in the tank—*what wuz I thinkin'*?! I managed to get filled up just outside the Connecticut-New York border by leaving my guitar with the attendant on the promise that I would duly redeem it on my return trip. And so I did, and so did he hand my guitar back to me, unscathed. Ahh, those were trusting times!)

The *chef* remained unmoved. Her *impossibles* were beginning to seem—dare I even think it?!—only too possible. In desperation I tried one final ploy—like Bret Maverick pulling a $1,000 bill out of his boot in order to see and call his poker opponent. I ventured to suggest that I had often heard it said there was nothing impossible in France, hoping this might stir within her the sense of a national tradition that she would be unwilling to contravene. It didn't; and it had become obvious that any more insistence on my part would be judged, probably correctly, to be in bad taste.

I surrendered. A noble myth had been exposed as just that and nothing more. I had no choice but to pack up my notebook and whatever non-library books I had brought with me, and head home. I got in the line where a library employee (in this case a work-study student) checked everyone's briefcases and duffel bags (I think backpacks were slow to catch on in Paris—perhaps the image of Quasimodo still haunted the students' imaginations), to make sure they—alas, *we*—weren't leaving with any unauthorized materials. As I passed by him he spoke to me, not furtively but blandly, as if we were just exchanging empty pleasantries, saying "I overheard your discussion with the *chef*. Next time you come, check out the book you want and I'll let it through."

"Why take the risk?" I asked.

"Because I like to put trust in people."

It would have been uncomfortably obvious if I had doubled back and come through a second time with the book in question, especially with the eagle watching us from her aerie, so I just hoped my new-found friend would be at his post the next time I came. And that he was still of a mind to place trust in a stranger—a foreigner, even.

He was, he did, I left with it, got it copied, brought it right back, and went on to become *the* authority on Claude Buffier in philosophical circles (if encyclopedia entries are any indication—I offer this as a minor footnote, and any of you readers in the "philosophy business" will recognize that it certainly should in no way be seen as a boast). Well, I confess there did happen to be a lapse of about 15 years between those first five acts and this final result. And so we see trust rewarded, but more importantly, *the impossible was again vanquished.* Long live the common wisdom!

But really, where in the adage does it say that the person who initially raised the specter of impossibility bears sole responsibility for laying it to rest?

DE GUSTIBUS

The eat-to-live vs. live-to-eat contrast between America and France is of course harsh and extreme—we Americans derive our share of pleasure from eating, just as the French are known to find enjoyment in activities best carried out elsewhere than the dining room. And yet beneath every leaf of exaggeration lurks an escargot of truth. My years spent in France sensitized me to the almost reverential attitude which the people of France held (and still do hold) toward food, its consumption and delectation. But the first intimation I was to receive of this attitude came several years prior to my ever visiting the country—prior, in fact, to my ever giving any thought to making such an excursion. (In the old B&W films that I love so dearly, the scene would at this point become blurry, and begin to spiral slowly into the background while a string of harp glissandos would lead us back . . . back . . . back . . .).

This intimation was packaged in an observation communicated to me by a 6' 8" fellow graduate student, who was giving a brief account of how he had spent his previous two years in "post-doctoral research." That 6' 8" modifier, incidentally, is not just a casual toss-in or an out-of-place space filler: it proves to be an axial desideratum in the anecdote to follow. The individual in question was not pursuing any formal post-doctoral program of the sort that has become quite common in recent years (a technique universities have devised in an attempt to squeeze a couple more years of cheap labor out of students before setting them loose on the job market)—he had simply decided to spend some time in Europe after the completion of his Ph.D., and before entering into competition for an academic position stateside (a competition, incidentally, that was a good deal more manageable then than now). The story he told went as follows.

One evening, while dining in a restaurant in France, he was approached by a couple young men, roughly his age or younger, athletic in appearance. His 6' 8" frame was difficult to tuck away and conceal in a small establishment, and the fellows who approached him were interested in knowing whether he played any basketball. This was in the late 1960s, and the sport was only then coming to enjoy a following in Europe; they were still a long distance away from developing the proficiency in the game that they enjoy now. Even in the 60s, though, they had semi-pro teams in Europe—perhaps along the lines of the (American-style) football team in Italy portrayed in John Grisham's *Playing for Pizza*, where no one—not even the owner!—got rich from it, but everyone was enriched by it.

My fellow student would have been quite a "find" for any such team back then. In addition to his size and skill, he had no academic obligations at the moment, no job awaiting his return two weeks hence, and no family yet that he was obliged to support. He was, in a word, free. (Hey, that really *is* just one word!) He agreed to join them for a trial run, and wound up spending two years with the team!

"But," I hear you muttering to yourself, "I thought I was settling in to read about how sacred the topic of the joys of the palate is to the French; not how the sport of basketball was incubating in the country." There are surprises for all of us along the way. Neither did our 6' 8" philosopher expect to be doing anything in the company of these young Frenchmen besides playing basketball. Yet the item that came right at the top of his account to me of what he encountered there had nothing to do with the respective skill sets of French vs. American players, the intensity that either brought to the game, whether they preferred zone defenses over man-to-man. It was, rather, to register his amazement at finding, in traveling with a collection of young, male, French athletes, how often their conversation came to focus on just one thing—and no, it wasn't *that* one thing: it was *food*. He said they could just go on and on in discussions of this restaurant or that, of one manner of preparing a certain dish over another, highlights of the cuisines of the many various regions of France. Basketball was just basketball—you find where and how you fit into a group fairly quickly, and take it from there. But the *après-game* conversations were where he really had a lot of refining to do.

For better or for worse, little interchanges of this sort can lodge in my mind for, well, apparently as long as I have a mind, because this one took place a half century ago. But his observation did keep surfacing through what was to become my decades-long attachment to the country. And most of what I was to see confirmed and reconfirmed this special devotion the French (at all social levels) have toward culinary delights.

Hear anyone French describe the vacation they just returned from, and odds are their first remark will be "*On mange bien* (or "*on ne mange pas bien*") *là-bas*"—"One does (or doesn't) eat well there." And this assertion, whether in its affirmative or negative version, lends its color to the remainder of the description. The natural scenery may have been beautiful, the people may have been warm and welcoming, but if the food they offered was substandard, well, why not try some place else next year? And if the food was excellent, hmmm, maybe a second visit just might turn up something interesting to see or do.

On the streets of any city or town in France you don't have to be rich, well-dressed or even marginally respectable to linger on the sidewalk outside a bakery or a *patisserie* and revel in the aromas that emanate therefrom. And at one time or another you will see people of all stripes doing just that. But these are far from the only establishments that contribute to the aromatic enticements of the sidewalk. Chickens as well as other birds roast in many shops right at streetside. Here in America as well, roasted chickens are widely sold, and yet they are typically cooked behind glass somewhere in the back of the store, and, when done, quickly packaged in plastic containers that do keep them warm, but also keep them from in any way interacting with our nostrils. It is almost as if some shame is associated with such a voluptuous odor!

Cheese, too, is sold here everywhere food is sold, but it will always be under clear plastic wrap—again, apparently, to spare us from ever actually getting a whiff of it. In France you can be led blindfolded down any street and know precisely when you are passing in front of a cheese shop (or a bakery, or a patisserie, or a fish market . . .). Delectation begins long before you actually sit down at a dinner table. And it can carry on long after the table is cleared: how many Americans have you seen kissing their fingertips in describing something they have eaten (or are about to eat, or are dreaming of eating)? It's a common gesture over there.

There are a couple celebrated French restaurants in the area where I now live (San Diego). Granted they are a cut above your above average steak house, and they do work to create an appealing ambiance that enhances your dining experience (the gustatory equivalent of waxen candles and incense in a church?), still when you get down to comparing dishes, preparations, you find that they are at best on par with the average Parisian bistro, the kind every neighborhood has a few of, often side by side—certainly nothing to compare with the vaunted Michelin-starred restaurants: just local eateries.

I made my way into this topic by talking about basketball, so let me pick up that thread here and carry it a bit further. Let's face it, America owns basketball. We own it the way England owns, uh, darts. Oh, there are a few players from abroad earning big salaries in our professional league, and every so often our team of all-stars will lose to some other nation in international competition, but the truth is, we have such a surfeit of basketball talent that the European leagues—now much more "serious" than they were a few pages back—set quotas for how many American imports any team can accommodate, otherwise their teams would be pretty much exclusively American. (That seems to bother them more than it bothered the National Hockey League, which for many decades consisted of only six teams, four in the U.S., two in Canada, while *not a single one* of the players was American born. I suspect there's a racist component to the European quota system, but there's no reason to pursue that here.)

Now it is important to note that the American players who head to Europe do so because they *aren't good enough* to play over here. And it seems to me to be much the same with regard to the great majority of the French chefs who come over here to set up shop. If they were really top notch, they would stay put and work their magic in a country that venerates culinary magicians, earn themselves a star or two in the Red Guide, instead of coming here to turn into something of an interesting side show. Granted this is not universally the case—some stars like Joël Robuchon or Alain Ducasse have seen the profit that comes from opening outposts in various major cities (New York, London, Las Vegas—I guess you can never make *too* much money)—but for the most part the rule applies. So I guess I'm saying that basically chefs of this upper echelon are the LeBron Jameses or Stephen Currys of France. The lesser practitioners who arrive on our shores have more or less fallen through the cracks in their own country—the Major Leagues—and while they do deserve respect over here, relatively speaking, they must have a sense of where they really stand in "the big picture."

Now inasmuch as dining is akin to a sacred experience among the French, it is crucial that in the presenting of a meal, nothing occurs that might disrupt the "spiritual" state of the diners. If, in a church service, the liturgy, music and general ambiance do not lead one into the appropriate attitude of contemplation and veneration, then the service itself becomes not a *celebration* of faith but a *test* of faith. So too a dinner must be offered in a manner that excludes any breath of negativity—joy alone should prevail. Consequently not only the repast itself but the manner in which it is served must be utterly exemplary.

There is a stereotype that exists—largely, it seems, in

American cinema—of the snooty French waiter. This, it appears to me, is a pure cinematic contrivance, one which enjoys no grounding whatsoever in reality. It might make for a laugh here and there, but honestly depicts nothing. The closest I have come to encountering such service has been here, when on rare occasions a waiter may become a bit too, as we say, "full of himself," for who knows whatever reason. But in my years spent in France I neither experienced nor witnessed any such conduct. (And in fact the American waiter has a rather extensive repertoire of offensive gestures, from the opening, faux-familiar "Hi, my name is Duane and I'll be your server," to his snatching of your plate out from under your fork just seconds after the last morsel has been consumed, to the closing mantra "then I'll bring you your check"—or worse, if you have paid with cash, "Should I bring you change?"(!))

In France a waiter is present to enhance your dining experience—certainly it is beyond his purview to pass any judgments on your suitability to dine within his establishment! I have ordered things that (French) friends around the table wondered about—an *entrée* and a *plat* both featuring creatures from the sea—*the horror!*—but if the waiter found it inappropriate, he kept it to himself. They will advise, if called upon to do so, but not insist, and certainly not volunteer any recommendation. I recall in the only three-star restaurant we ever dined in (which merited no more than two stars, but who am I to say?), the other man in our party of four was French, from Burgundy, hence knew a thing or two about wine. Once a decision had been reached among us as to what we would order, he called upon the sommelier (among the serving cadre sommeliers are something like our Army's Special Forces), and negotiations began as to what wine would be selected. They went on, and on—two men putting their heads together, affably yet in dead earnest, to arrive at the Greatest Common Good, as if they were readying themselves to sign an international trade agreement, and not simply uncork a bottle. The result of their deliberations, I must say, was the most powerful and exquisite white wine I had ever tasted, but the deliberations themselves were quite fascinating.

A waiter in France remains distant until you need something. Perhaps a person gives off little signals suggestive of some lack or want, prior to making an overt request (or maybe it's all transmitted via pheromones!), because they so often appear from nowhere in anticipation of your request. One time we dined at a very elegant spot on a small island in a small stream (where an old, abandoned mill still stood) down in the Perigord region. The day had been hot, and we were dressed for the day, but as evening advanced and a light breeze lifted off the water my wife started to feel a bit of a chill. I may have asked if she wanted my jacket (which I would have loved to get out from under), but she declined.

Then within moments of our little exchange, a voice emerged from behind us: *"Est-ce que . . . "*—a classic beginning of an interrogative sentence; it contains no real content but it does indicate that a question is to follow, and of course that someone nearby is asking it. *"Est-ce que madame aimerait une châle?"*—"Would madame wish to have a shawl?" But in fact no answer was awaited, or more likely the answer was already known in advance, as the shawl was gently being wrapped around her shoulders in the very asking of the question. It was the proprietor of the restaurant himself, who looked after certain of the needs of the patrons, and who must have detected from his post that a discomfort existed which required immediate attention (perhaps a common problem in that particular locale, since the means of remedy was close at hand).

I heard, in that tone of voice, in the manner in which it gently emerged from out of the silence, something of the deference a servant of earlier times would have shown to his master. Here, of course, in this modern world, the client had become master, but the sound was unmistakable. It didn't exactly please *me*—the anti-aristocratic American—but on that chilly, dewy evening at water's edge my wife welcomed it unhesitatingly with gratitude. And now that I think of it, I find the tone and the approach vastly preferable to that chirpy "Hi, my name is Duane."

Nowhere, however, are the differences in style more noticeable—differences between the "sacred" approach in France and, the secular, commercial attitude prevalent over here—than in the presentation of the bill. Duane asks "Will there be anything else?" and if the answer is negative, then either he tells you "I'll bring your check right away," or he just brings your check right away. And of course once it is there in front of you, why not just pay it and leave? ("But Duane, I thought we were such good buddies!?") But in France when it becomes clear that nothing more is to be ordered, the waiter makes one further act of transcendence—from the realm of the merely distant to that of the virtually invisible. And should his ectoplasmic apparition manifest itself across the room, making eye contact with it becomes a major challenge, and a daunting game of peek-a-boo commences.

The messages are clear in both cases. The American style says "Your time is up. I can make no more money from you. Please step aside so the next paying customer can occupy this table." And yet dining with a clock ticking over your head brings pressures that are antagonistic to the kind of a fulfilling experience that a French restaurant aims to provide. Their style, instead, says "We are pleased you have come to share a meal with us; rest assured you may remain at your table for as long as is comfortable, and let us not sully our relationship with talk of money."

I remember one evening putting this attitude to a serious test (not intentionally, it just happened that way: I hadn't yet formed hypotheses), as there were four of us at table, two who had a lot of catching up to do, two who needed to be introduced around—a delightfully complicated scenario. We talked and ate and talked, then ran out of things to eat, but not of topics to talk about, so on we went. The restaurant gradually emptied around us until we were the last patrons in the house, which in France implies that it was no earlier than midnight. No doubt the workers would have liked to be released from their duties and set free themselves on what was left of the night. So at a certain point our waiter headed over to our table . . . . . and with a smile presented us with a cool, fresh bottle of Evian (no charge), as he could see we had talked ourselves hoarse.

How could we refuse it?!

And so, Duane, I suggest you do a little traveling on your next vacation—call it a busman's holiday—and pay a visit to the country which venerates food and food service, where you can enjoy *and* learn and enjoy some more, all at the same time. I don't know who has been teaching you up to now, but perhaps with the right exposure you will undergo some form of, shall we say, *spiritual conversion*. And maybe on your return *I will be telling you* to keep the change, and not reacting grumpily to an unsubtle attempt on your part to extort it from me. Stranger transformations have occurred over there, I can assure you.

SKETCHBOOK

People can hardly be separated in our consciousness from places, nor places from people. Certain people permeate a place for us as the warp and weft sustain a carpet; others shine forth from it like a jewel embedded, while yet others command our attention as does an unwanted snag or a coffee stain. Often people are taken to be "representative of" a place—the paradigmatic Californian, Parisian, southerner. I take this to be rather risky business, though, as all too often a stereotypical image winds up lopping off traits or attributes that are interesting for their very atypicality. Personally, I seem more drawn toward what we might term the *radical individuality* of a person, rather than what accords with any general image of a "type." This puts me at odds with much of modern science, ranging from the rigorous to the "softer" approaches. I get the distinct impression, for example, that my doctor sees me as little more than an agglomeration of statistics, a numerical hologram perched, at the moment, or that seems to be perched on the edge of his examining table. A sociologist will focus on a different set of statistical parameters, but in either case too much individuality or eccentricity—and it doesn't take much to reach *too* much—cannot be countenanced. I have seen minds slammed shut right before my eyes when I happened to raise some question about personal individuality or—worse!—uniqueness.

Not surprisingly, then, the *singularity* of someone,

or perhaps even the singularity of a brief encounter with someone, is what burrows deepest into my own memory. To me (*pace* Shakespeare's Antony), the *special* that men do lives after them; the *common* is interred with their bones. A few of the people I encountered in Paris across the years left some such deep and lasting impression with me, and it is to them that I pay faint homage now.

None enjoyed the slightest measure of celebrity. (Of celebrities, I did cross paths with a surly looking Tony Curtis once, up near the Place Vendôme, and Gerard Depardieu was holding forth on the sidewalk outside a café one evening. And I'm *sure* that was Brigitte Bardot who zipped past me in a little powder blue car—after all, the driver was blonde and the car had *Fondation Bardot* inscribed on the side of it—what more evidence could be required?! But these aren't the people who concern me here. The workman who stopped me on the street to ask where he could find the *Allée des Sycamores* comes close, as he seemed a bit less interested in really finding the street than in showing me that he had been called to do some work on Sylvie Vartan's plumbing; but this was just *too* brief an encounter.) All those whom I remember here came and went (or will soon go) without stirring up a ripple on the surface of the great city. But each left a mark on the city-for-me. The reader will pardon me, I hope, if I betray an occasional touch of sentimentality in the following pages. Rest assured it is only a passing condition—there is still plenty of acerb left in my tank.

Napoléon IV

There is little chance that the concierge in our building would be deemed, taken, or mistaken for a "typical Parisian"—he was Portuguese in origin, came north for work at some point, and stayed. That said, I am reminded that my Japanese roommate of an age ago once brought out a magazine from his home country, containing a 20-question quiz aiming to determine "How Japanese are you?" We both took it, and I proved to be decidedly more Japanese than he was. So I guess anything can happen. (But I still wonder, how Japanese was it that, when he was elected president of the Japanese Society at school, his first order of business—*seriously!*—was to disband the Society? And there was no second order of business.) I have heard, from time to time, that the subset of Parisians consisting exclusively of concierges should be characterized as "a breed apart." But even if this were true, I have no doubt that *our* concierge was one of those mutations of that particular breed, whose eccentric DNA had in some mysterious way been orchestrated into the Larger Plan in order to assure some measure of species variation.

I have read—and it wasn't on the internet that I read it, so it has a chance of being true—that the system of concierges that lives and reigns in Parisian apartment buildings was initiated by Napoléon. And he did not do so for the convenience of the residents—to assure they received their mail and had their various needs attended to—but rather out of distrust of them. The concierge was in fact a plant, a spy, a pair of eyes and ears put in place to ferret out any intimation of social unrest that might have been smoldering within the walls, so that it could be properly "dealt with." If this was the case, then in a perverse way it was unfortunate that Napoléon, or for that matter the Empire, was long gone, and could no longer reap any benefits from *our* concierge, for no one could have been more on top of the goings on—*all* the goings on—in our 104 unit complex than Monsieur Dos Santos. However, absent any such overarching power to report to, and yet with a vast storehouse of "dirt" at his fingertips, at some point, apparently, it occurred to him that he could put all this knowledge to his *own* use: "Who needs Napoléon, anyway? Let me *be* Napoléon!" And so in the microcosm that was our building he adopted the persona of the Little General, strutted about in its tiny courtyard as if it were the garden at Fontainebleau, and maintained a working order among all of us, his devoted if occasionally disgruntled subjects, all the while exacting tributes from same.

He kept a notebook. In it was recorded every service he provided to every individual in the complex, and every compensation he received in return, all of which had to be expressions of our "gratitude," as there were no set fees for any of these services (he already received an adequate salary). In addition, around Christmastime a holiday gratuity was expected from us, even if he had done nothing for a person individually besides "his job," and it too would be inscribed in the notebook. So suppose you were in the habit of giving him 200 francs each year at this time, and for some reason you cut that back to 100 francs one year—maybe it was just a tough year for you financially. Some note of that shortfall would be made in the little book, and a reprisal of some form would be sure to follow. Perhaps it would take the form of the non-delivery of mail (which I suspect is a federal offense there as well as here), or the refusal to sign for a package (thus forcing the recipient to trek to some far away depot to collect it), or denying, to anyone who inquired at his window, that a particular individual actually resided there. There no doubt were other ruses up his long sleeve by which he could punish the ungrateful, but these happen to be the ones I know of, *because at one time or another he did all of them to me.*

I knew of this notebook because—and only because—he told me about it. Otherwise it seemed to be a closely guarded secret. Now this revelation came, not on my arrival, but only after a number of years of coexistence, during the initial portion of which I am certain that my page was written in livid scarlet. We—*I*—started off rather badly, and while I did over time win my way into his good graces, thanks to some advice from people conversant with the "system," this reversal of fortune did not come overnight. My problems derived, quite simply, from my taking him to be a person like me. (And to think, I started this little piece extolling people's individual differences. But a word of advice here, dear reader: whatever type of person you may be, we really aren't all alike. You egomaniacs—it is not the case that *everyone* is at all times looking out exclusively for *numero uno*. Manipulators—we're not all *working you* for some hidden something. But most importantly, you good and caring souls—keep a sharp eye open for those other two types I just mentioned.)

Our concierge was most affable early on, at least that's the way it seemed. Shortly after arriving I discovered I couldn't gain access to our little subterranean cellar space (a wretched area, with half a century of cobwebs enriched by half a century of airborne Parisian pollutants dangling perilously overhead), due to a lock the previous owner had left on the door. Our concierge very graciously fetched his hacksaw, attacked the lock, and within a couple minutes had made his way through one of its arms, allowing the door to swing wide open. I would have been content, incidentally, to do the sawing myself, if he would but have left me in charge of the saw for a bit, but he seemed to throw himself so eagerly into the task that I demurred.

Now if I had rendered a simple service of this sort for someone else, I would have taken mild offense if they offered me not thanks but money for my troubles: "You don't think I could help you out . . . just because you needed helping out?" Here, though, I found myself face to face with a quite contrary mentality, and at the moment I didn't realize that this was the case. As it turned out, there was a *quid pro quo*, which in fact more closely resembled *quidproquo*. Even so, I did tuck it in the back of my mind to reward him with a little something at Christmastime. But Christmas was only too too far away! Some time later, after the various acts of hostility mentioned above had been committed, I described my mini-plight to a friend, who inquired if the fellow had done me any particular favors, and when I described the hacksaw event to him, he saw right away that money should have flowed immediately from me to the concierge, upon his completion of the task. As undignified as this seemed to me, whenever any such occasion arose in the future, that's what happened. And from then on we all lived happily ever after.

Well, eventually. Wounds require some time to scar over, so "eventually" was a while in coming. Still the time did arrive when he would greet us, after our long stays away, with a genuine warmth, as we had slowly moved up on his psychometric scale from impudent foreigners to endearing ones. I think, in fact, he may have confided to me about his notebook and its contents, along with other details about his life past and his life to come, in large part because of this—because I simply was not part of the flow and ebb of daily Parisian life, only alighting into it occasionally (though rather predictably--the way the coots arrive here in Mission Bay in December and head north in March, or the black skimmers in April, heading god-knows-where a few weeks later). That is to say, once we "fell into line," our otherness seemed to become not so much an occasion for hostility but a genuinely attractive feature.

And it must be admitted, he did run a tight ship. Matters pertaining to business were handled with dispatch; and any potential malefactors who happened through our gates were quickly ushered out into the street again. When he finally retired we came to appreciate him even more, as his replacement was hardly as efficacious and surely not so colorful.

The couple times we did cross paths on the street, subsequent to his retirement, we greeted each other like old friends. To be honest, I doubt that would have been the case with most of the other residents there. To all appearances, time had swallowed all traces of The Notorious Hacksaw Incident. (Time and a salubrious transference of money!) Even now I wonder, though: Could that wicked little notebook still be out there somewhere?!

La Bonne Samaritaine

Labor strikes are not nearly as uncommon in France as they are here. In the U.S., the tight alliance between corporate power and government—the Union to end all unions—has left workers increasingly defenseless, while increasingly perilous economic circumstances have rendered them more fearful of reprisals. So they seem largely to have surrendered stoically and silently to forces that lie beyond their control.

I Don't Like to Complain

Not so in France: their innate feistiness provokes outbursts of resistance, outbursts which rarely last all that long (though the trash collectors' sit-down went on, like, *forever*—or so it *seemed!*), yet which enable the workers to make their presence felt—and who knows, perhaps they even derive a bit of enjoyment from the fact of making their presence felt. Most frequently it is one, some, or all of the various transportation systems that are in this manner afflicted. And since public transportation is much more widespread, efficient, and *relied on* there than it is here, its interruption produces large-scale disturbances—especially, of course, in the more densely populated areas.

During one such disturbance we decided to make our way across town. I no longer remember why we did so, but occasional buses and trains were running, we had no particular "where" to be, hence no "what time" to be there, so perhaps we just set out to see where chance would lead us. Little did we suspect (indeed *not at all*) where that would be!

Since we were setting out from the outskirts of the city, we at least managed to find a seat on one of the rare buses that was heading east, toward the center. In no time, however, the bus filled up to the point where retaining one's seat became rather ludicrous, so we stood like vertically packed sardines until we reached the point of transfer, then we exited. But what transfer? We soon gave up on any notion of profiting further from public transportation; naturally the sidewalks were curb-to-wall people, all of whom had likewise abandoned hope. And of course whoever had a car was in it, so traffic was reduced to a crawl, at best.

When we had finally reached wherever it was we were going (I just hate myself for forgetting where that was!), and had turned around to head home, I calculated that we had probably 3 1/2 miles still to cover. With the late spring day being on the warm side, my feet and legs were not eager to take on that challenge. But one must do what one must do, so off we went.

We hadn't gone far, though, before a car pulled up to the curb beside us, and a woman opened her window and spoke to us. More precisely, she spoke to my wife, who was a couple feet closer to the roadway than I was. In fact I may well have been more than a couple feet distant from her at that moment, because I couldn't hear what was being said, plus I didn't appear to have been included in the initial overture. For what the lady had asked was whether my wife would like a ride . . . a ride to wherever she was going. When the driver learned that I was going to have to be factored into the exchange, she seemed to hesitate a bit, perhaps thinking she had bitten off more than she should be attempting to chew. But she quickly relented—what could she say? "Not enough room"? The car was empty. "Can't take a chance on a strange man"? Well, the woman she was inviting along had.

Now let me interrupt this narrative here to pose a question. Suppose you were walking down the street in a comparable American city—of course there are no American cities comparable to Paris, but I have heard some New Yorkers refer to their city as "Paris-west" (*Dream on!*), so imagine, if you will, that you are walking down an avenue in New York, a car pulls up beside you, and the driver asks you if you would like a ride to wherever you would like to go. Here are some possible responses that you might make to that proposition: (a) Get lost, creep! (b) Get serious! (c) Uh, no thanks (laughing dismissively). (d) No reply—you just move to the building side of the sidewalk and quicken your pace. Or for that matter put yourself in the driver's seat—would you really invite any complete stranger on the streets of New York to get into your car? If you answer this in the affirmative, well, there's a cell on Rikers with your number on it, waiting for you. But Paris is different. The lady stuck to her offer, even including me, I climbed into the back seat and off we went.

She was reacting to the chaos of the day by taking to her car and seeing if she could help someone make their way home in a less stressful manner. That someone turned out to be us. The ride was a rather long one, both because we lived out by the edge of the city, and because the traffic was understandably dense (we might well have been able to walk the distance faster, but were delighted not to have to). The conversation flowed freely between us (I suppose she found our "story" a bit more interesting than that of the ordinary quotidian commuter). When at last we arrived at our street I think we were all feeling some slight regret that this little adventure was about to come to an end.

But then it didn't. The lady asked us whether we had ever been to Chamonix—the glorious resort town that lies at the foot of Mont Blanc. We hadn't. Then she asked if we might care to spend a week there. Free of charge. In a small inn that we would have to ourselves, save for the caretakers. Who would fetch us from the train station and ferry us back to town. (!!!) Apparently she was a rental agent of sorts, knew that particular spot would be vacant (it was the *entre deux saisons* period, after skiing but before hiking), and so capped off our little escapade with an offer we couldn't refuse.

The transportation systems must not have returned to

a completely normal state when we headed for Chamonix, because we missed our train. But we did catch the next one, rearranged with the caretakers, and all was well, for ending well. Now I still wonder: Did *any* of the transportation workers (or for that matter any other of their "victims") profit vaguely as much from that strike as we did?

Un Modest Coiffeur

That is how the gentleman introduced himself to the merchant up the street from him: *"Je ne suis qu'un modest coiffeur"*—"I'm just a humble hairdresser." The phrase remains lodged in my memory, perhaps because it had the ring of having been formulated long in advance, or maybe it sounded like a line straight from a du Maupassant story. Whatever the reason, it is inseparable from the hairdresser's story. And the "humble" posture was one he assumed for *our* (slight) benefit, and not at all for his own.

He operated what is usually called here a "beauty shoppe" (is it *ever* written without that "-pe" at the end?), and it was situated on one of our regular routes, hence we passed by it once or twice daily. In the window of the shop a few objects for sale were on display—some scarves and a little costume jewelry—though they had probably been placed there more for decorative purposes than commercial. But it so happened that my wife took a liking to one of the scarves, and wound up buying it. And that is where our little story begins.

Since we were nearing the end of our stay for the year, and as the item had a fairly hefty price tag attached to it, we thought of circumventing the substantial sales tax that they have in France (on certain goods it can exceed 20%), through a process known simply as the *détaxe*. Many a tourist goes through this process, and the larger department stores are well prepared for it, with stacks of the necessary documents at the counter, and somebody nearby who knows how to fill them out. The gentleman we were dealing with, however, possessed neither the relevant documents, nor, if he had had them on hand, the expertise to fill them out. His clientele, after all, was overwhelmingly local, and most of his "product" wasn't even taxable, consisting principally of perms, trims, and a flood of compliments. So it was not surprising that he was ignorant of the mechanics of the *détaxe* system.

What *was* surprising was the way he threw himself into the task of finding out, for the benefit of someone he had no previous dealings with, and with whom he most likely would never have any again. I expected he would just shrug off our request, for even though it is in some sense required of any merchant to prepare the necessary paperwork, lacking the necessary documents was a fairly good excuse not to do so, and of course the international customer hardly negotiates in such a matter from a position of strength. I expected, in short, to just pay the price and let it ride.

But our humble hairdresser would not have it that way. He was determined to do right for us, whatever that took. And so with the cheeriest demeanor, chatting liberally about his visit the previous year to Montreal (*practically* the same country as ours—at least it's in the same time zone!), he and we headed up the avenue together, to a shop where we knew the owner was properly informed about the *détaxe* system.

The shopkeeper there was equally accommodating (perhaps *détendu* by that little "humble hairdresser" intro, though it should be noted that he was not obliged to stir from his own premises in this transaction), and together they produced a document that would satisfy the agents at the border. We accompanied the gentleman back to his little establishment, thanked him, bade him adieu, and went away once again marveling at the good-natured hospitality—far beyond whatever the "call of duty" might have dictated—shown us by one of those "irascible Frenchmen." One, in this case, whose name we never even came to learn, though whose *métier* will forever stand out.

The Song of Roland
All I wanted was a T-shirt with a little *caché* to it—that's not an extraordinary wish, or one that implies any excessive vanity on my part, is it? I wasn't looking to find anything that had, in George Costanza's unforgettable phrase, "caché up the yin-yang." In fact in the realm of T-shirtdom, I'm not quite sure what that would involve: "M.I.T. RUGBY CLUB"? "CHERNOBYL HOCKEY MOM"? No, the one my eyes had with pleasure fallen on read simply, in two half circles, "CHALET DES ILES" [upper arc] "BOIS DE BOULOGNE" [under arc].

I was pleased to have the deep connection to France, to Paris, that I had come to have, and T-shirts are often how we Americans celebrate our (at times esoteric) connections. But there were none at any of the stands I visited that proclaimed anything like, say, "JE PAIE MES IMPOTS," though paying one's taxes is definitely a way of "being part of a place" (somewhat the way we used to say of a local deli proprietor back in Boston who suffered from psoriasis, "there was a little bit of Sidney in each of his sandwiches"). Shirts mentioning the Sorbonne (none of whose wearers ever attended there), or emblazoned with Eiffel towers and triumphal arches were sadly commonplace—caché-free, one might say. But I knew immediately that the Chalet-des-Iles one would be unique (even in Paris!), because it was never sold anywhere. It constituted simply a part of the "uniform" of certain workers associated with that establishment—a divine little bistro situated on one of two tiny islands that sit in the middle of a slightly less tiny lake in the Bois de Boulogne, the huge park that constitutes much of Paris' western extremity. The workers we had become acquainted with, however, were not restaurant-related, but were involved in another activity that somehow fell under the same management: the renting of rowboats.

Boating on the lake (the *Lac Inférieure* by name, a name which it came by despite being the larger, prettier, and more popular of the two lakes, simply by being lower in elevation than the smaller, less significant one that fed into it; a similar account, incidentally, stands behind our own Lake Superior) has been an established pastime since the lakes were carved out of a marshy area back in the time and under the aegis of Napoléon III. For us, though, a rowboat was something we saw in our future back home, so we took advantage of the opportunity there in Paris to give my wife the chance to develop some finesse in propelling and manipulating a boat with a pair of oars. Somehow this activity caught the attention and the imagination of numerous Parisians walking along the water's edge, as we had to have been photographed a good half dozen times while my wife rowed and I luxuriated on the rear seat (or as an old tar might have put it, on the "aft thwart"). Even a policeman was one of those photographers! When I noticed him I thought perhaps he wanted something, or that we were in violation of some mystery ordinance, but when I looked questioningly at him he communicated to me, through a most expressive explosion of hand gestures: *"Pay no attention to that man in uniform holding a camera!* Just continue what you are about." So we did. I still wonder if that snapshot at one time went up on a precinct bulletin board somewhere.

We took out a subscription for access to the rowboats, any day any time, for a month, though we only took advantage of it every few days, and normally went early in the morning to avoid unruly crowds. On most of our days there we shared the lake only with an elderly gentleman who feathered his oars beautifully, and was accompanied by his dog, and a lady in a broad-brimmed, lacy hat and white gloves. The man in charge, with whom we did our dealing, was one Georges Roland, a good-natured fellow who carried out his little job with no pretenses. It struck me, actually, that this was probably the last job he would have, perhaps the final refuge he would enjoy before a life on the streets. For better or for worse, this is not the way things turned out.

We got on very well with one another, and in fact the only reason I came to know his name was that he asked us, when we departed, to send him a post card that captured something of the area where we lived, which we were happy to do. But I'm a little ahead of myself here—it's too soon to be departing.

Toward the end of our subscription period I finally summoned up the courage to ask him if he could come up with a T-shirt for me, of the same sort as he and the other workers there wore. He indicated it was indeed possible (why would I have thought otherwise?!), and I assured him I would pay whatever price he suggested, but he would have none of that. Just the same, my wife wouldn't let him off that easy, and made it known she would prepare a tray of brownies to be shared by him and his couple assistants.

So a day was set when the exchange was to be made—brownies for T-shirt. We toted them up (the mile plus) to the boat launch; Mr. Roland was there with the shirt I had been questing after . . . and he had a second one, as well. That one was for my wife, who had never figured into the negotiations, but who was now receiving a T-shirt *that was way prettier than the one I had just been presented with!* Typical Frenchman—I should have expected it!

On top of that bonus shirt, however, he also insisted that we have a bottle of wine that he had brought for the occasion. It was of a type that I had not encountered before—a Coteaux de Lyonnais—and given Mr. Roland's humble station in life, we had our doubts about its excellence, or even its potability. But when some time later we got around to opening it, we found it remarkably tasty, much like a top-of-the-line Beaujolais. After doing some research, I located the shop in town that dealt with this particular vintner, discovered that they made deliveries, and from that time forward the Coteaux de Lyonnais was formally established as our "house red."

We returned a year later to take another spin in one of "our" rowboats, and renew our acquaintance with Mr. Roland, but were saddened to learn that my impression about that being his terminal employment had proved true. Not, however, because he had been let go, but because in that short, intervening year, he had died. Suddenly a boating excursion on the Lac Inférieure was no longer the lark we anticipated it would be.

I have no illusions about the truth of the adage that nothing is forever; and yet it still feels that some things are altogether too brief.

IDLE-IZE ME!

The trauma of relocation bears with it a thousand grinding labors and a hundred fond regrets—people and places to be seen no more forever—all, in this case, on the promise of "something better," which may or may not prove to be so. But in coming to southern California, specifically San Diego, more specifically La Jolla, amid this swarm of labors and losses, there did emerge one sweet moment of pure, undiluted joy—like unto the passing of a kidney stone. That came the day I sold my lawnmower. And the joyousness of this occasion was only enhanced by the fact that it came in mid-July. For we were shortly to depart on our journey westward from Kentucky, and each and every Kentucky July brings with it either boiling heat, or drenching storms, or searing drought, pummeling all the inhabitants and making of the month, year after year without fail, a study in meteorological misery. And whatever misery every person suffers simply going about the business of everyday life is painfully augmented for those who, once a week, are obliged to push a lawnmower through the unrelenting grass.

In every household in central Kentucky (the region known *ironically* as "The Bluegrass," since bluegrass actually fares very poorly in that climate—*what doesn't?!*), there is someone who is responsible for carrying out such a chore. And in our household that someone was me.

It was just something one did. My next-door neighbor was a former Chief of Police—a well-respected man in Lexington and justly so (a true gentle man, although I would have advised taking a closer look at those salt water taffy-shaped candies in the cut glass dish there on his coffee table before taking a bite out of one—actually they were bullets!). But regardless of his stature in the community, he mowed his own lawn. And when he became too old to be pushing a mower safely (in that July heat), and given the distinguished position he enjoyed among his fellow citizens, he took the only honorable step that one in his circumstances could take: he bought himself a riding mower.

But my joy was unrestrainable that one July day, because as deeply ingrained as this same impulse had become in me—29 years deep, in point of fact—I nevertheless knew, and took delight in the knowledge that it would no longer hold sway over me. No more would I be pushing that infernal machine, for we were soon to be part of a community in which all the grass grew on what was designated as common property, and all the mowing of it was contracted out to a lawn care service. An era had ended. I was free at las', great *God amighty* free at las'!

Over time, though, I came to recognize that in this divine little town it wasn't just the private communities where lawn care was placed in the hands of outsiders—virtually *every patch of grass* was maintained by someone who arrived in a rickety pick-up bristling with hoes and rake handles and redolent of eau de two-stroke-engine cologne. I would bet that an inventory of all the garages in all the houses in all of La Jolla wouldn't turn up more than a handful of lawn mowers, most of which sat perpetually idle, each having probably accompanied its owners in a move from some easterly state--owners who could no

Idle-ize Me

more leave it behind than they could the family dog!

I came to see, also, that much more sat idle out here than just a few displaced lawnmowers. Mobile dog-grooming outfits seemed to survive, if not thrive. Don't feel like washing your own dog, but can't bring yourself to pack her into the car and bring her on down to our shop? Not a problem—we'll bring the shop to your front door.

Find it tedious to stand around for five minutes (next to God knows who!) while your Ferrari goes through the car wash? Not a problem: our to-your-garage-door car wash and detailing service spares you the hassle of actually driving—just back your car into the driveway and we'll take care of the rest.

But my eyes were opened wider yet when, toward Christmas time, signs started appearing on fences, lampposts, etc. advertising "WILL HANG YOUR CHRISTMAS LIGHTS FOR YOU" (!!). Why, Clark Griswold (that "saint with children and genius with food additives") hung all his own Christmas lights, even though the total wattage commanded thereby would have exceeded that of a medium-sized town. Yet it turns out those same signs go up year after year, indicative that people actually do pass on to others the responsibility for fulfilling what was once a personal chore.

Well, this one got me to thinking. There must still be avenues—or at least alley ways—open to provide services to people who heretofore had not realized they needed them, but who in the future will not be able to do without them. So I offer here a few ideas whose time may be just about to come, starting with a Christmas-themed one.

"WILL OPEN YOUR CHRISTMAS GIFTS FOR YOU." Shopped until you dropped? Give not a further thought to actually dismounting from your couch and dragging yourself over to that beautifully decorated tree to fetch your gifts. Just give us a call, and as you sit in your living room contentedly gazing at this tree, one of our highly trained technicians will bring all your gifts to you, one by one, right to the sofa you sit on. Then to avoid your suffering any nasty paper cuts, she will open them and lay them out within easy reach. The rest will be up to you.

"WILL DELIVER YOUR MAIL." Of course the postal service is thoughtful enough to bring your mail to your *address;* but then they just stuff it in a box. Out by the street! We will make sure that it makes that final leg of its journey, from mailbox to your front door. Sometimes it rains, after all. Why take the risk? Call today to arrange a delivery time convenient to you.

"WILL BRING YOU YOUR NEWSPAPER." Who knows where that scatter-armed paper boy will fling it next?! Under a bush? *In* a bush? Maybe up in the rain gutter, on a day when he's "really feeling it." We are committed to retrieving your paper wherever it finds its way to on any given day, and delivering it to your doorstep. (And we also offer our blue-ribbon service, where a trained reader will skim through the headlines for you and highlight those articles that appear worth reading.)

It is with a certain reluctance that I offer these suggestions to the public. For while they are intended merely to indicate the direction my thinking has been carried, upon my introduction to this new region and novel way of life, who knows, they might point the way to future commercial successes which I may one day wish (need?) to exploit. So it could well be painful to me to see, one December day, an "unwrap your Christmas gifts" sign posted on a nearby fence, bringing with it the realization that my innovative scheme had been stolen right out from under me. But in the interest of self-revelation, that is a risk I am hereby taking.

THE OLYMPIC EXPERIENCE

Number crunchers, stat freaks—for two weeks the Olympics buried us under an avalanche (no, wrong metaphor—this was the *summer* games), a *flood* of firsts,mosts, longests. Happily our (America's) gross medal count enabled us to find a relatively simple parameter to claim "We won!" However, it certainly looks as if the British were the winners, as they—a nation of 1/5 our population, nevertheless collected medals roughly equal to 2/3 of our total. Let's see now, do we multiply across and divide diagonally, or is it vice versa? Long ago, and far away. What we do is convert everything to decimals, that's what, and take it from there. So if we were to have brought home a share of medals proportionate to the British, we would have needed 335, not the paltry 104 we did garner.

But wait! On this method of accounting—the per capita method—the really big winner would have to be Granada, who with their one gold medal and roughly 100,000 population would oblige the American contingent to come back with a shade more than 3,000 medals. Gold ones! Tuck those flags away, fellow citizens; we've been humbled by . . . Granada. What goes around, comes around. Could it be time, perhaps, for another invasion?

But there are more numbers to come to grips with, e.g., most points scored by an American basketball player in one Olympics, breaking the record held by Spencer Haywood. *Spencer Haywood?!* Are any of you old enough to remember *him*? Back when he played, there were few people, in fewer other nations, who even knew how to dribble! Then of course there is Michael Phelps, and his trophy case brimming with medals of all colors. But while we're at it, why not tote up the number, say, of inscrutable hand gestures made to the audience by very tall sprinters? (We may have to review the tapes a few times to get a handle on that one.) And do they ever put a watch on those victory laps the runners take? I can hear it now: "Mohedyn narrowly missed setting an Olympic and world record in the 5,000, but he then steamed around the track, country's flag in hand, a good three seconds faster than Bikila's 1996 mark." And did you know the average person, over the course of a lifetime, will swallow four spiders in their sleep? Oh wait—how did that get in there?

But one number stands tall above all other measures of Olympic prowess, and makes us realize that for two short weeks the world thrilled to the accomplishments of some Truly Exceptional Individuals (who seem to have enjoyed a thrill or two of their own, away from track, pool or court). And the number is this: 100,000. And that number represents the number of condoms supplied to London's Olympic Village.

***100,000*!!**

Oh there goes the math again: Let's see now, just how many athletes were there? How long was the stay of each of them? Sha-**zaam**! Let loose the torrent of snarky jokes and double entendres—no sense *my* engaging in any and spoiling your fun. (It was just the same a couple years ago: remember how difficult it was to come across anyone who *didn't* have a quick, salty jab at Tiger Woods ready at hand?)

I bring this up, though, not to marvel at the exploits

of these world-class athletes, but to register my sense of indignation. For you see, only last summer I was a participant in the San Diego Senior Olympics competition, and I look forward to repeating the experience next month. And at that event we were all presented with a little complimentary sack of swag consisting of, well, of various things—the arm of the advertisers reaches far and deep. But I could swear that I came across nothing vaguely resembling the item highlighted above. There was of course the obligatory T-shirt, destined to be stuffed into the deepest recess of the least used drawer—we were all there, after all, to relive a bit of our past, to pretend at being college kids again, not to be cruelly reminded of our Senior status. (Perhaps they could take a hint from the *San Diego Reader*, a local weekly, who awarded me, as a prize for solving Sudoku puzzles--a T-shirt saying *San Diego Reader Surf Team*, which I wear proudly. Presumably they figured: "What dork would want to go around advertising that he was a Sudoku-meister?!").

Then let's see, there was a little rubber gizmo that you use when your grip has become so feeble that you can't twist open a jar—doubtless a jar of some joint-lubricating ointment, or perhaps one of those pill bottles with a "child-proof" cap (child-proof indeed! Your basic child would be in and out of it in a few seconds, but I have to hunt down the vice grips to wrench it open). With this rubber pad, though, you just put it between your hand and the jar lid, give it a spin and presto! On the pad was printed the name of some health insurance company, clearly questing after our business, hoping we would choose them as a Medicare supplement. The only other freebie I remember was a towel the size of a washcloth—come to think of it, maybe it *was* a washcloth—that had the name of some assisted living facility emblazoned on it (which made its way to the same drawer as the T-shirt).

So here's my plea: How about it, San Diego? Get with the program! Show a little respect for your athletes. Slip a little "surprise" into *our* sack this year. One can only hope there are a few left over from the Olympic Village. I'd recommend that you check with Overstock.com.

www.ingramcontent.com/pod-product-compliance
Lightning Source LLC
Chambersburg PA
CBHW070448050426
42451CB00015B/3397